Careers in Biotech and Pharmaceuticals

2006 Edition

WetFeet Insider Guide

WetFeet ®

Helping you make smarter career decisions.

WetFeet, Inc.

The Folger Building
101 Howard Street
Suite 300
San Francisco, CA 94105

Phone: (415) 284-7900 or 1-800-926-4JOB
Fax: (415) 284-7910
Website: www.WetFeet.com

Careers in Biotech and Pharmaceuticals

2006 Edition
ISBN: 1-58207-530-1

Photocopying Is Prohibited

Table of Contents

Biotech and Pharmaceuticals at a Glance

Opportunity Overview

The demand is high for scientists with backgrounds ranging from molecular biology and biochemistry to combinational chemistry, informatics, and statistics, and for scientists with management experience. In genomics, jobs are particularly plentiful for scientists who produce proteins and for bioinformaticists who have both science and computer skills.

- You don't have to have a science background to work in this industry, but it helps. Those with BS and MS degrees and some lab experience can enter as research associates; those with a BS or BA can land jobs as pharmaceutical field sales reps (especially if they have some sales experience). Manufacturing is a good entry point into the biotech industry because you'll receive training and interact with people working in many other areas. Although a PhD is your best bet for long-term success in the industry, those with a BS or MS and skills in the latest technologies, such as microarray scanning, will find a strong job market.

- MBAs can find a variety of jobs in finance and marketing, but jobs in business development are harder to come by without industry experience.

- PhDs usually come in as associate scientists.

- Many types of engineers—chemical, electrical, industrial, or mechanical—find ample opportunities in manufacturing, process development, and R&D.

- RNs and other medical professionals can find opportunities as clinical research associates, and pharmacists can apply their experience to marketing divisions.

- MDs usually work on companies' clinical trials, typically for consulting fees or other forms of compensation. Most doctors tapped for such duties have significant clinical and research experience and solid professional reputations.

Major Pluses

• You work for a company whose products can improve or save lives, and sometimes even eradicate terrible diseases.

• Choose your own adventure: Those who seek stability and structure can find it in pharmaceutical firms; those pursuing a wilder ride can sign up with a small biotech outfit.

• For scientists, the industry offers an alternative to the low pay of academia; for MBAs, it requires fewer hours than consulting or banking demands.

Major Minuses

• Though your work can help save lives, the bottom line almost always comes first.

• After a period of consolidation, Big Pharma no longer offers ironclad job security. The industry has also been rocked by several controversies.

• Very few potential drugs make it from conception to market. This is particularly significant if you want work for a small biotech shop whose business depends on the success of one or two products.

Recruiting Overview

Biotech and pharma weathered the economic downturn of 2001 better than many other industries. The industry produced a string of blockbuster drugs that led to solid revenue increases and a need for more workers. The upward trend has continued: new products, revenue growth at a number of companies, and job openings for the right candidates. One caveat though: Recent concern about the safety of some drugs could affect the industry's financial performance and job prospects.

The more technical your skills, the better.

The best way to get the attention of recruiters is to know someone on the inside. Get out there and network. A good place to start is with members of your school's alumni association who work in the industry and who may be able to make invaluable referrals.

If you don't have experience, consider starting with a job in one of the larger companies, which tend to be good training grounds. Even if you think you'd prefer the more entrepreneurial environment of biotech, a couple of years in the world of Big Pharma can help you better understand the industry's big picture.

- **Undergrads:** Companies in this industry don't typically recruit aggressively on campus. A good option is to get a temp-to-perm job through an employment agency that specializes in science and technology. Don't rule out biotech manufacturing, where you can demonstrate your potential and learn more about the business from the inside. If you want a job in sales, try networking through your school's alumni association and look in local papers and on company websites.

- **MBAs:** Companies recruit at a few core schools; contact your career center to find out who recruits at yours. Otherwise, work hard to find a personal connection on the inside.

- **PhDs:** A lot of recruiting goes on via networking. Talk to your professors to find out whether they know people in the industry with whom you might schedule an informational interview.

- **MDs:** Headhunters play a significant role in recruiting MDs. A number of search firms have practices—sometimes run by doctors—that focus on recruiting physicians. And don't hesitate to contact the human resources department of any company that interests you.

The Industry

Overview

The pharmaceutical drug discovery and development industry has grown to become one of the most profitable in the world. During the last 30 years, the industry has blossomed, with billions of dollars spent on research in biochemistry, molecular biology, cell biology, immunology, genetics, and information technology—and billions of dollars in profits earned by drug companies. Indeed, in 2004, the pharmaceutical industry sold $550 billion in pharmaceutical products worldwide.

But the process that turns this rich research into medicines that can help patients is a slow and often heartbreaking one. It now takes an average of 12 years and $500 million to nurture a drug from initial discovery through FDA approval. Despite the billions of dollars companies spend every year on drug development, the FDA approves only a handful of drugs each year. Each stage of development is fraught with high failure rates; even when a company has proven the efficacy and safety of a drug through a prescribed series of clinical trials, there's still a 25 percent chance its drug application will not be approved by the FDA. Despite the odds, though, the prize is grand enough for the few who hit the blockbuster-drug jackpot that an ever-increasing number of companies is willing to gamble that their product will be the next to reach $1 billion in annual sales.

The industry can be divided into two broad categories: pharmaceutical companies and biotech companies. Pharmaceutical companies make medicines from plant- and chemical-based compounds. Biotechnology companies seek to duplicate or change the function of a living cell to make it work in a more predictable or controllable way. (Pharmaceutical companies also produce livestock feed supplements, vitamins, and a host of other products, and there is an entire field of biotechnology that uses genetic technology for food and agricultural purposes, but the industry's nonpharmaceutical applications are not covered in this Insider Guide.)

Though formulating medicinal compounds is an ancient practice, the U.S. pharmaceutical industry as we know it began when companies developed large-scale manufacturing processes during the 19th century. Biotechnology, on the other hand, is a relative newcomer; the first companies formed almost a century later, in the 1970s, and the first biotech drug brought to market—human insulin produced in genetically modified bacteria—was not approved by the FDA until 1983. Born out of Watson and Crick's 1953 discovery of the structure of DNA and Cohen and Boyles's 1973 success in transplanting a single piece of DNA from a toad into a bacterium, biotechnology uses genetic research to develop products for human diseases and conditions.

Pharma and biotech employ people from all sorts of backgrounds for all kinds of jobs. Scientists with undergraduate degrees, MAs, and PhDs work in research and development, as well as in quality assurance and quality control to ensure that all products meet federal safety standards. Engineers, in diverse areas of specialization, work to design processes for manufacturing drugs and automating elements of the research process. Physicians design clinical trials to evaluate the safety and efficacy of new drugs. Computer programmers build systems to model molecular structures and create massive databases. Salespeople convince doctors and other medical professionals, managed care organizations, and government agencies to give their companies' products preferential treatment. MBAs also have plenty of opportunities. Those working in finance track the movement of the vast sums of money that are borrowed, made, and spent both within a company and around the industry. Others create and execute marketing plans for established and fledgling drugs. And in business development, MBAs compete for the rights to ideas and technologies that might give their firms an edge in the race for the industry's Holy Grail: an FDA-approvable, marketable compound that gives patients relief without unpleasant side effects.

Though job opportunities in pharma and biotech largely mirror each other, there are notable differences between the two. Because many biotech firms are still developing their initial products, they are much more focused on research. This means jobs for nonscientists are more scarce in biotech than in pharma. Biotech firms tend to expand their marketing and sales forces when—and if—a viable product nears FDA approval. And it's become common for small companies to seek alliances with larger companies that already have the requisite infrastructure in place for these functions.

Another difference between pharma and biotech is size. In 2003, the entire biotech industry spent $17.9 billion on R&D, whereas the top five Big Pharma companies alone spent nearly $32.6 billion on R&D in 2004. And the largest pharmaceutical firms employ as many as 100,000 people, while Amgen, the largest biotech company, had 14,400 employees at the end of 2004. This means that pharmaceutical companies tend to be more structured and hierarchical—more corporate—than biotech firms, which generally have a more chaotic, egalitarian, and improvisational work culture.

Regardless of these differences (and sometimes because of them), there is a growing convergence between pharmaceutical and biotech companies. Big Pharma often provides the bucks and/or sales force necessary to help little biotech bring its technology to market. Amgen had the early support of SmithKline Beecham, and the Swiss company Roche Group has a majority stake in Genentech. On the other hand, the small biotech organizations have the agility and pioneering spirit to spawn the new generation of research that can breathe vitality into the product pipeline of an aging pharmaceutical company. This can result in mutually compelling alliances among competitors who must negotiate tricky issues of economic survival versus independence. For every partnering success, there are stories of uneasy bedfellows, with some noisy public court cases as evidence.

Biotech and pharma have been performing exceedingly well relative to other industries in recent years. The appetite for blockbuster drugs that can address medical ailments and keep people young is insatiable—the latter a reflection of the aging baby boomer population. International markets have also blossomed. The future looks bright.

Yet Big Pharma has encountered rough waters over the past year, especially related to a relatively new and very popular class of drugs known as COX-2 inhibitors. Most notably, Merck has been beset by problems related to its popular antiarthritis drug Vioxx. In 2004 Vioxx was pulled off the market after some studies suggested a link between Vioxx and increased risk of heart attack and stroke in some patients. In February 2005, the FDA gave Merck the go-ahead to return Vioxx to market, but as this Insider Guide went to press, Merck was facing lawsuits filed by at least 4,600 people or their survivors.

The world's largest pharmaceutical company, Pfizer, faced its own COX-2 troubles. In late 2004, Pfizer announced that its blockbuster arthritis treatment Celebrex could increase the risk of various heart ailments. Celebrex generated $3.3 billion in sales during 2004 for Pfizer. In April 2005, the FDA and European regulators ordered Pfizer to stop selling Bextra, another COX-2 inhibitor. Not even Viagra, the much-ballyhooed impotence drug, was safe. In 2005, the FDA launched an investigation into whether using Viagra could lead to serious vision problems.

Bristol-Myers Squibb paid approximately $300 million to settle a criminal investigation by the Justice Department into alleged accounting manipulation from several years ago. The New York company has also struggled in recent years to introduce successful new products while cutting costs and reducing the size of its sales force. Bristol-Myers has seen its stock plunge about 60 percent since 2000. The industry has also continued to face criticism about genomics, pricing, and patent practices.

Regardless of whether you choose to work for Big Pharma or small biotech, don't get too attached to the status quo. These days, the business environment can change overnight. One need only look at recent biotech stock volatility for ample evidence of that. And as one insider says, "Even in Big Pharma, if there's a merger or a spin-off, you can easily find yourself without a job."

The Bottom Line

The pharmaceutical job market is healthy. While Big Pharma is under attack for its pricing and patent practices, it is among the most profitable industries in the United States. Biotech, on the other hand, relies on the public and private funding markets to survive the long years until a product is approved for sale; insiders advise that you ascertain whether your prospective biotech employer has at least 2 years of funding, and preferably more, in the bank.

In demand are people with scientific backgrounds, particularly those with that rare combination of science and computer skills required for bioinformatics, as well as those who combine scientific training with managerial ability. Folks with BS or MS degrees in chemistry, molecular biology, genetics, biochemistry, computer science, and physics can find absorbing careers. However, a PhD is required if you want to advance beyond the level of research associate. Nonscience undergrads can get a foot in the door in biotech manufacturing or pharma sales. MBAs who forgo consulting and investment banking careers will find a more palatable work/life balance along with good pay and some of the best benefits packages around. MDs can find well-paying, engaging work that offers regular hours and is free of managed-care administrivia.

Above all, those who choose to work in this industry enjoy the very real satisfaction of knowing that they are laboring to produce drugs that could make a radical difference in the lives of thousands, even millions, of people.

Industry Breakdown

BIG PHARMA

Insiders refer to the handful of multinational giants that dominate the industry as Big Pharma. The majority of Big Pharma companies are headquartered in the United States, but several are based in Western Europe—Switzerland, Germany, and France. Those headquartered in the United States are all located east of the Mississippi, with the greatest concentration in New Jersey.

A few years ago, a wave of consolidation engulfed this industry, with already-giant companies merging into even larger companies. One example was Pfizer's acquisition of Pharmacia. One driver for consolidation is that patents on a significant number of blockbuster drugs, such as Paxil and Imitrex, have recently or are about to expire. When patents expire, the market is opened to competition from lower-priced generic versions of the drug. Sales can drop by as much as 80 percent, leaving drug companies scrambling to pick up the slack. While some look to consolidate resources through mergers and acquisitions, others believe that signing pacts with biotech is the best way to shore up their product pipelines.

Big Pharma companies come in two styles: diversified and nondiversified. Diversified companies, which include Johnson & Johnson, Abbott Laboratories, and Wyeth, maintain other health care–related businesses, such as consumer health product divisions and medical device companies, while those that are nondiversified—Eli Lilly, Merck—focus solely on the development and sale of drugs. Over the past few years, some diversified companies chose to divest their nonpharma concerns in favor of the leaner and more profitable drug business. Bristol-Myers Squibb, for instance, sold Clairol, the number-one hair-products company in the United States, to Procter & Gamble in 2001.

BIOTECH

Despite the success of such biotech giants as Amgen and Genentech, a large majority of biotech shops are still small enough for everyone to know everyone else's name. But a growing number is joining the elite group of biotech firms that have FDA-approved drugs on the market; in 2004 the FDA approved 224 new biotech drugs produced by biotech and Big Pharma firms. Once a biotech company has reached the stage at which it has a product coming to market, its jobs expand from the primarily science-focused to include marketing, manufacturing, engineering, and sales. Culturally, companies tend to have growing pains as they move from R&D to commercialization, but their organizations tend to remain much leaner and flatter than those in Big Pharma.

Even with 1,444 biotech firms employing some 137,000 people in the United States at the end of 2004, the biotech industry is significantly smaller than the pharmaceutical industry. Still, this is a vibrant sector. Revenue for the industry increased to $54.6 billion worldwide in 2004 (for publicly traded companies), up 17 percent over 2003. The industry recorded a net income loss of $5.3 billion, an increase of $700 million over its net loss in 2003. Only 67 of the 330 publicly traded biotech companies in the United States were profitable in 2004.

Though funding for biotech concerns dropped in the early 2000s, this remains one of the industries where investors are most likely to put their money. Indeed, according to the PricewaterhouseCoopers MoneyTree survey of venture capital (VC) investments, though down from a peak of $4.25 billion in 2000, VC investment in biotech companies was strong in 2004, at $3.96 billion for the year, up from $3.50 billion in 2003. The first quarter of 2005 was weaker. Venture capitalists invested $632 million in 68 deals, down from $917 million over the same period in 2004. Still, that represented about one in every ten VC investments.

Biotech companies tend to be located in geographical clusters, often near prominent research universities. The largest concentration of biotech companies is in California (in and around the San Francisco Bay Area and San Diego, mainly), followed closely by Massachusetts. You'll also find pockets in such far-flung regions as Washington, D.C.; Raleigh-Durham, North Carolina; and Boulder, Colorado.

While the mapping of the human genome accounts for a lot of the press the biotech industry has enjoyed in recent times, the real key to curing gene-based disease is to understand the function of the proteins that these genes encode. The study of proteins and their post-translational modifications, called *proteomics*, is a hot field. Another hot field is nanobiotechnology, which combines biotechnology and nanotechnology (the study of super-small structures and machines as tiny as one molecule). To support postgenomic research, powerful new tools have been designed, such as microarrays for evaluating proteins on a massive scale, high-pressure liquid chromatography, mass spectrometry for microsequencing and purifying protein, and bioinformatics software for collecting and analyzing data.

A number of scientists and engineers are finding opportunities to broaden their career paths by working for companies that design and market postgenomic tools and instrumentation. For example, there is a need for scientists who can provide training and technical assistance to the scientific customers who purchase these tools. The computational demands of the new postgenomic data will be enormous.

Industry Rankings

Key Pharmaceutical Companies

Company	2004 Revenue ($M)	1-Year Change (%)	Employees
Pfizer	52,516	16.2	115,000
Johnson & Johnson	47,348	13.1	109,900
Bayer AG	40,310	12.2	113,825
GlaxoSmithKline	39,032	2.1	100,019
Novartis AG	28,247	13.6	81,392
Roche Holding	27,630	9.9	64,703
Merck & Co.	22,939	2.0	63,000
AstraZeneca	21,426	13.7	64,000
Sanofi-Aventis	20,377	101.4	96,439
Abbott Laboratories	19,680	0	60,600
Bristol-Myers Squibb	19,380	−7.2	43,000
Wyeth	17,358	9.5	51,401
Eli Lilly	13,858	10.1	44,500
Takeda Pharmaceutical	10,284	17.8	14,592
Schering-Plough	8,272	−0.7	30,500
Astellas Pharma	4,839	14.5	9,062
Teva Pharmaceutical Industries	4,799	46.5	13,800
Forest Laboratories	3,114	17.5	4,967
Organon International	2,694	−5.6	15,000
Allergan	2,046	15.5	5,030

Sources: Hoover's; WetFeet analysis.

Key Biotech Companies

Company	2004 Revenue ($M)	1-Year Change (%)	Employees
Amgen	10,550	26.3	14,400
Genentech	3,980	42.2	7,646
Biogen Idec	2,212	225.6	4,266
Genzyme Corp.	2,201	28.4	7,100
Serono S.A.	2,178	17.2	4,740
Applera Corp.	1,825	2.7	5,360
Chiron Corp.	1,723	−2.4	5,400
Gilead Sciences	1,325	52.6	1,654
MedImmune	1,141	8.2	1,976
Covance	1,056	8.4	6,700

Sources: Hoover's; WetFeet analysis.

Top Therapy Classes

Therapy Class	2004 Revenue ($B)	Global Market Share (%)	1-Year Change (%)
Cholesterol and triglyceride reducers	30.2	5.8	11.7
Antiulcerants	25.5	4.9	1.4
Cytostatics	23.8	4.6	16.9
Antidepressants	20.3	3.9	1.3
Antipsychotics	14.1	2.7	12.1
Antirheumatic nonsteroidals	13.1	2.5	3.3
Angiotensin II inhibitors	12.0	2.3	22.1
Calcium antagonists	11.6	2.2	1.6
Erythropoietin products	11.4	2.2	8.9
Antiepileptics	11.3	2.2	17.7

Source: *Pharmaceutical Executive* (www.pharmexec.com).

Industry Trends

PRICING

Insiders say this may be the biggest issue the industry currently faces. Who will pay the cost of drug development? As more treatments become available, will only the wealthy have access to them?

Prescription drug prices are rising annually, while insurers are getting increasingly stringent about which medications they'll reimburse their customers for. Exciting new drugs can cost thousands or even tens of thousands of dollars per treatment. Providing price relief for seniors has been an issue for several years. Many favor price controls to prevent costs from skyrocketing, a move the pharmaceutical industry opposes.

The pricing battle is international. South Africa was among the countries to sell drug knockoffs. In 2001, 39 pharmaceutical companies filed a lawsuit to prevent South Africa from buying knockoffs of drugs that are still under patent protection. Drug companies contend that they must protect their patents because this is the only way they can generate sufficient revenue to pay for the continued research that leads to the discovery of new medicines. (Critics respond by pointing out that the pharma industry spends far more on marketing than on R&D.) Pharma companies were hit by a wave of bad PR as a result of the lawsuit, which was soon dropped. After negotiations, pharma companies started selling drugs in Africa below cost. While this might solve one problem of access, it has put more pressure on the industry to maintain its pricing structure elsewhere in the world.

O CANADA

Many patients have been responding to high drug prices (many of the newer drugs on the market carry a price tag of $175 per month or more) by buying drugs at lower cost from other countries. Canada is the country in the spotlight these days, as it ships a high volume of pharmaceuticals to patients in America. But importing prescription drugs is illegal in the United States—and, according to the FDA, unsafe. The pharma companies hate this trend, of course, because their profits will suffer if people can buy drugs at cheaper prices than the drug companies charge in the United States.

Some Canadians are worried that selling drugs to American consumers will create short-ages. In mid-2005, the Canadian health minister said he would introduce legislation to ban the bulk export of drugs to the United States. He also said he would create a system to monitor more closely drug supplies in the country.

In the United States, legislators are pushing to legalize the import of prescription drugs over the Internet from Canada. A number of lobbying organizations in the United States, meanwhile, have criticized Big Pharma on behalf of their citizens, who, they say, should be able to buy drugs at the lower prices they can get by importing them.

STILL MORE ETHICAL AND LEGAL CONCERNS

The biotech and pharmaceutical industries have lately faced wave after wave of bad press. Environmental proponents have gathered evidence to support their claims that biotechnology-produced foods are unsafe, and their protest has gotten louder.

Meanwhile, drug companies have come under fire for some of their clinical trials practices. Many drug companies test their drugs overseas, in poor countries where it's easier and cheaper to recruit test participants. The question on the mind of critics is, What do drugmakers do when their tests are over? In many cases, test participants received medication that vastly improved their quality of life. Should drugmakers be able to cut off the supply of the drugs they're testing once those tests are complete? Is that ethical? Should drugmakers be obliged to provide the drugs in the poor countries where they've run their tests once the drugs have gone to market? Companies are grappling with these and similar questions. Some have marketed drugs in poor countries where they were tested, but with so few in those countries able to afford the drugs, it's a money-losing proposition. Regardless of how much they grapple with this ethical quandary, don't bet on drugmakers doing anything that will even remotely threaten their bottom line.

Drugmakers have faced criticism for, in effect, buying influence with state and federal government officials. For example, in early 2004, some U.S. senators called the National Institutes of Health (NIH) to task for allowing its scientists to accept consulting compensation from pharmaceutical and biotech companies.

Similarly, a number of drug companies have come under fire for driving the creation of new state drug guidelines used by state-run health facilities. The problem? These guidelines seem to invariably direct state-employed physicians to prescribe expensive new drugs being sold under patent by the very companies who, in effect, wrote the state prescription guidelines.

Finally, some claim that one of the dirty secrets of the drug industry is that many expensive new drugs don't really work that well. According to these critics, most prescription drugs work only part of the time and many can have potentially serious side effects. And in many cases, there are older, cheaper drugs available that could help many patients as well as newer, more expensive drugs, without the potential side effects of the newer drugs. Yet the drug companies, with their armies of salespeople, are able to create interest in new drugs among physicians (who don't have the time to really study the claims supporting the new drugs), and those physicians then prescribe those drugs in lieu of traditional alternatives.

THE HUMAN GENOME MAP

. . . may finally be yielding some bottom-line results. The interesting thing is that, so far, the benefits the pharma and biotech industry is receiving from the human genome map is not in the form of new drugs, but rather in the drug-testing process. Companies like Merck and Millennium Pharmaceuticals have used DNA chips, or gene expression arrays, to weed out bad drugs earlier in the development process. The hope is that this technology will allow companies to cut the development cost for new drugs, which currently averages $500 million. A bit farther down the road, companies hope to benefit from the new technology by targeting specific patient populations for whom specific drugs would work best.

LET'S MAKE A DEAL

Because the cost of soup-to-nuts drug development, manufacturing, marketing, and sales is prohibitive, a growing number of biotech companies that once dreamed of competing on equal terms with Big Pharma now instead seek partnerships. Indeed, last year, there were 502 alliances between pharmaceutical and biotech firms. The trend is expected to continue. About three in four of the 126 biotech companies with less than $500 million in revenues surveyed by Deloitte & Touche said they would increase the number of their alliances over the next 3 years.

The nature of these alliances varies: In some instances, a biotech shop exchanges an exclusive license to market and sell a patented drug to a pharmaceutical company that is willing to pay some research costs up front. Such agreements may also include limited use of the pharmaceutical company's manufacturing and distribution channels.

In other instances, a pharmaceutical company makes a cash investment in exchange for a portion of future revenue, an equity stake in the biotech partner, or both. This type of relationship is often tied to a marketing and distribution deal like the one described above. As a result, it's not unusual for Big Pharma to have biotech holdings that give them a substantial piece of the action.

TROUBLE IN PARADISE?

There's a dearth of new drugs coming to market these days. In 2004, the FDA approved just 21 new drugs, down from 53 in 1996. Why? Industry observers point to a number of possible reasons. For one thing, the genomics revolution has not been as successful as biotech companies and their investors had hoped it would be—at least, not so far. For another, a decade or so ago, pharma companies changed the way they discovered new drugs. Instead of letting lab scientists do what they'd always done—which included exploring their hunches—they took to creating thousands of chemical combinations and testing their drug potential using robots. This was supposed to be a faster, cheaper way of finding new drugs. Instead, it's turned out to be an ineffective means of drug discovery.

Meanwhile, with key patents expiring or set to expire in the near future, biotechs and pharmas are facing increasing pressure to come up with new marketable products, since investors demand that companies' growth charts must point ever upward. The result is that pharmas and biotechs alike are focusing on squeezing more and more revenue out of fewer and fewer drugs.

This is driving the spate of alliances across the biotech and pharma landscape. Biotechs and pharmas alike are seeking existing drugs that they can license. Pharmas are seeking to license drugs from biotechs that may not have the financial and professional muscle to market them so that they reach their full sales potential. Biotechs are seeking to license nonblockbuster drugs that their Big Pharma developers don't want to spend time and energy promoting or researching for new indications when that time and energy would be better spent helping potential blockbusters reach their full sales potential.

So, currently, pharmas and biotechs alike are focusing more on licensing drugs that other companies have developed, and focusing less on developing brand-new drugs. Obviously, this scenario is unsustainable; eventually, a steady supply of new compounds will be necessary for these industries to maintain their profitability.

The Drug Development Cycle: A Case Study

Drug development runs along a predictable sequence. Understanding that sequence is key to getting a good sense of how the industry works. With that in mind, we offer the saga of Gitajob (generic name: initiativudine), a promising new agent from Damptoz, the large pharmaceutical arm of the diversified global powerhouse WetFeet Worldwide.

2004   Damptoz R&D isolates a compound that appears to hold promise for treatment of slackerosis, a psychiatric syndrome found most commonly in young adults and characterized by depression and heightened levels of cynicism. Because no slackerosis treatment is currently on the market, Damptoz decides to explore its viability as a compound for development. Scientists set to work exploring the compound and conducting animal testing to study its safety and efficacy. At this point in its lifecycle, Gitajob hasn't even been assigned a generic name; it is known wholly by internal control number DTZ-2104. Animal test results are mixed—rats and mice become more focused on assigned tasks in their cages, but other animal data is inconclusive. Despite misgivings about DTZ-2104's ultimate prospects as a successful drug, Damptoz continues to move it through the product pipeline. Staff chemists and chemical engineers evaluate various ways to get the compound into a deliverable form (in this case, how best to turn it into a pill) that can be manufactured cheaply. Other engineers set to work figuring out the best chemical methods for mass-producing it.

2008   The regulatory affairs department submits an investigational new drug (IND) application to the FDA to indicate the imminent start of human clinical trials. Because the IND makes the compound public information, WetFeet Worldwide registers a patent. All patents on a compound last for 20 years, during which time the patent holder has exclusive rights to all of its commercial applications.

2009   Clinical trials commence. Over the course of several years, they progress from Phase I, in which fewer than 100 people are enrolled, to Phase II, in which a few hundred people participate. Phase III usually requires a placebo-controlled, double-blind study (some patients get the drug, others get a sugar pill identical in appearance, and neither doctor nor patient knows whether the drug or the placebo is being given) to ensure that initiativudine can effect a greater clinical benefit than the placebo. The Phase III work ultimately involves 1,300 patients on three continents, selected at random to be either drug or placebo patients. Due to harmful side effects or ineffectiveness, 19 in 20 drugs don't make it through clinical trials.

2015   The compound makes it through Phase III! The regulatory affairs department submits a new drug application (NDA) to the FDA. The application is 40,000 pages, a bit shorter than average. Several of the supervisors in regulatory affairs are taking a gamble that the FDA will make good on its promise to require less paperwork when processing NDAs. If the gamble fails and initiativudine gets labeled "nonapprovable," a subsequent NDA will cost Damptoz millions of dollars in the short term and, based on time lost on the product's patent life, probably tens of millions in the long term. If another manufacturer has a competing drug that is also close to approval, the losses could be substantially higher.

After much agonizing and countless quantitative marketing studies, the sales and marketing departments set the pricing for Gitajob and construct a marketing strategy. This includes deciding which direct-to-consumer (DTC) and/or professional channels to use for advertising, the design of visual aids for salespeople to use when they detail, and the presentation of the drug at professional conferences. For 3 years the marketing division of Damptoz has been conducting elaborate market research, identifying the physician specialties most likely to prescribe it, as well as when: first-line, before a patient has tried any drug treatment for slackerosis, or second-line, after a conventional antidepressant shows no benefit after 3 months in use. The marketing team interviews hundreds of likely patients, asking them if they would consider a drug for their condition and how much they would be willing to pay for it out of pocket and via a prescription plan. The marketing folks also need to find out how best to address Gitajob's unusual primary side effect, which is urine discoloration in 30 percent of patients. Moreover, a small number (3 to 6 percent) of asthmatics reported seizures while taking Gitajob. Are the apparent benefits of the brand a fair tradeoff for these risks?

The pressure to maximize revenues is huge, because all of the hundreds of failed drugs that don't make it through development have to be financed by blockbuster drugs. Chemical, mechanical, industrial, and process engineers in manufacturing have moved into high gear to get the compound into production in Damptoz factories worldwide. The Asian market, notably Korea and Japan, is clamoring for the drug to be sold there, but tariff complications have slowed the approval process and the Japanese government is threatening to omit the drug unless Damptoz cuts its wholesale price by 23 percent. Can Damptoz reps detail the drug to doctors anyway? And if it's officially illegal to do so, how steep are the penalties?

2016   The FDA approves the compound for prescription use to treat slackerosis in teenagers, but not adults, because a handful of fraudulent patient records were uncovered by FDA audits of adult patient charts at two study centers. As a result, Damptoz can only promote Gitajob (its brand name is now in use) as a treatment for teens; any attempts to portray it as useful in adults will be much frowned upon by the FDA. (Even though the fraudulent charts numbered only four of a sampled 52, in a study where total patients enrolled was in excess of 1,300, all of the study data is now suspect and the burden of proving it to be legitimate belongs to Damptoz.)

2028   Gitajob, though not the blockbuster Damptoz had hoped for, has racked up billions of dollars in sales. It's a good thing, too, because the patent expires this year, which means that a number of generic drug companies will put out their own formulations of initiativudine (Damptoz gets permanent rights to the original brand name). Demand for Gitajob will drop precipitously; the generics, which are chemically identical to the branded agent, sell for 70 percent less than Gitajob. But Damptoz still has a few tricks up its sleeve. The company has already begun to market (and of course patent) a new, extended-release version of the drug, which will be sold under the name Gitajob XR. Where standard Gitajob must be taken every 8 waking hours, Gitajob XR needs to be taken only once daily. In addition, the company has submitted applications to the FDA to convert the drug from prescription to over-the-counter status. If the application is granted, Damptoz will be able to ply Gitajob on drugstore shelves nationwide and capitalize on its brand recognition.

The Companies

ABBOTT LABORATORIES

100 Abbott Park Road
Abbott Park, IL 60064
Phone: 847-937-6100
Fax: 847-937-9555
www.abbott.com

It all started in 1888, when Dr. Wallace Abbott succeeded in developing the specific formulation by which medicine extracted from plants could be administered in very precise doses—Abbott called the little pills he'd created "dosimetric granules," and they were so successful he began selling them to other practices. Now, Abbott Labs, with more than 60,400 employees worldwide, is a multibillion-dollar company that spent $1.69 billion on research and development in 2004. The company distributes its products in 130 countries directly or through representatives.

Among its major products are Depakote, for the treatment of epilepsy, migraines, and bipolar disorder; the anti-infective Biaxin (the patent for which expired in 2005); TriCor, for the treatment of elevated triglycerides; Synthroid, for the treatment of hypothyroidism; Mavik and Tarka, for the treatment of hypertension; Meridia, for the treatment of obesity; the antivirals Kaletra and Norvir, protease inhibitors for the treatment of HIV infection; and Humira, for the treatment of rheumatoid arthritis. Humira generated $850 million in sales in 2004. Abbott's biggest-selling drug in 2004 was the acid-reflux treatment Prevacid ($3.8 billion), which is made and sold by TAP Pharmaceutical Products, a joint venture between Abbott Labs and Japanese drugmaker Takeda Pharmaceutical.

In June 2002, Abbott's diagnostics division aligned itself with genomics information company Celera, in a strategy to increase its presence in the genetic testing market. The two companies are working on a testing platform for early detection of viral and genetic diseases, especially HIV, hepatitis C, and cystic fibrosis. Though the alliance does not include licensing agreements, Abbott's large sales and marketing network will help both companies profit from collaborative patents.

Not all the recent news has been good at Abbott Labs, though. In July 2003, the company announced it was taking a charge against earnings to settle a probe into alleged marketing and insurance misdeeds.

Company insiders say the company is very team-oriented. Typically, Abbott fills anywhere from 2,000 to 5,000 positions each year. This number covers all of Abbott's divisions and includes new positions and positions open as a result of retirements and turnover.

Recent Milestones

2005   Abbott ceases selling the attention deficit drug Cylert, citing declining sales. The drug also came under fire from a consumer advocacy group, which said Cylert caused 20 cases of liver failure.

2004   Abbott spins off its hospital products business Hospira.

In July 2003, Abbott Labs defends a 400 percent price hike for its AIDS drug Norvir, the FDA chastises it for portraying the drug as the lowest priced of its kind and for failing to adequately disclose risks associated with the drug.

Named to *Working Mother*'s list of the "100 Best Companies for Working Mothers."

In a survey by *Science* magazine, named one of the "Top 20 Employers" among biotech and pharma companies.

2003   Purchases coronary stent business from the JOMED group.

2002   Receives FDA approval for Humira, a rheumatoid arthritis drug with blockbuster potential, and Synthroid, a synthetic thyroid hormone replacement therapy.

Key Financial Stats

2004 revenue: $19,680 million
1-year change: 0 percent

2004 global pharmaceutical revenue: $13,756 million
1-year change: 11.6 percent

Personnel Highlights

Number of employees: 60,600
1-year change: 16.1 percent

ALLERGAN, INC.

2525 Dupont Drive
Irvine, CA 92612
Phone: 714-246-4500
Fax: 714-246-4971
www.allergan.com

The name Allergan is pretty much synonymous with Botox—the name of the anti-wrinkle treatment that has created a sensation among aging celebrities and society-page types. Botox works by temporarily paralyzing the facial muscles and usually costs $250 to $500 per treatment. The procedure has to be repeated every few months. Sales of the drug were $705 million in 2004, beating expectations and accounting for more than one-third of the company's revenues. (In 2003, the drug had $564 million in sales, accounting for 32 percent of the company's total revenue.) Allergan is even running clinical trials to explore other possible uses for this drug, such as pain relief for migraine headaches. Eye care pharmaceuticals accounted for $1.1 million of the firm's revenue.

Botox is Allergan's first major drug. In general, the company's strategy differs from that of other pharma companies: Instead of relying on revenue from a few very successful, widely marketed drugs, Allergan does its business mostly in the specialty markets of ophthalmology, neurology, and dermatology. Eye care products alone—including medications, surgical equipment, contact lenses, and intraocular lenses—make up some two-thirds of the company's sales. Because it's carved out these unique niches and built brand recognition as the leader in these categories, Allergan doesn't have to allocate as much money to big marketing campaigns, and it doesn't have to compete with other pharmaceutical companies jockeying for a piece of the hottest markets.

Insiders say that Allergan encourages competition among employees; if you want to move up the hierarchical ladder here, you're going to have to shine.

Recent Milestones

2004   Spins off Advanced Medical Optics but agrees to manufacture its products until mid-2005.

Licenses development and marketing of several ophthalmic drugs in Japan to Senju Pharmaceutical and Kyorin Pharmaceutical.

2003   Is warned by the FDA that its Botox advertisements are misleading, downplay the drug's risks, and promote the drug for uses for which it has not been approved.

Sued by Klein-Becker, maker of StriVectin-SD antiwrinkle cream, which alleges that Allergan used strong-arm tactics to try to suppress the "Better than Botox?" advertising campaign for StriVectin.

Acquires Oculex Pharmaceuticals and Bardeen Sciences Company.

2002   Announces that its eye care and pharmaceuticals divisions will be divided into separately traded companies.

Key Financial Stats

2004 revenue: $2,046 million
1-year change: 15.5 percent

2004 global pharmaceutical revenue: $1,842 million
1-year change: 5.0 percent

Personnel Highlights

Number of employees: 5,030
1-year change: 2.0 percent

AMGEN INC.

1 Amgen Center Drive
Thousand Oaks, CA 91320
Phone: 805-447-1000
Fax: 805-447-1010
www.amgen.com

Amgen is the largest of the biotech companies. Thanks to its 2003 acquisition of Immunex and strong sales growth, Amgen has entered Big Pharma territory with revenues surpassing $10 billion in 2004. Indeed, it brought in more global pharmaceutical revenue in 2004 than Big Pharma stalwart Schering-Plough.

Amgen specializes in protein therapy for disorders of regulatory cell growth, such as cancer and neurodegenerative disease; Immunex was strong in rheumatoid arthritis and leukemia therapeutics. The company counts several blockbusters in its portfolio, including Epogen, which combats the anemia that frequently accompanies AIDS; the immune system-stimulator Neupogen; and Enbrel, a new arthritis-treatment drug, co-marketed with Wyeth, that came to the company with the Immunex acquisition. Other drugs include Neulasta, to treat chemotherapy side effects; the anemia drug Aranesp (basically, an improvement on Epogen), which Amgen hopes will become a $5-billion-per-year drug; and Kineret, a drug that treats rheumatoid arthritis. In 2004, Epogen generated $2.6 billion in sales, more than a quarter of Amgen's sales.

While Amgen is a leader among biotechs because it has successfully transformed from a revenueless start-up into a successful drug marketer, the company remains R&D-focused. Indeed, in 2004, it spent $2.0 billion on research and development.

According to insiders, it's worth it to get in the door here—the culture is reportedly collegial and the benefits excellent.

Recent Milestones

2005   Makes *Fortune*'s list of the "100 Best Companies to Work For."

2004   Spends $1.3 billion to purchase remaining shares of Tularik, which has five drug candidates in clinical trials. Before the purchase, Amgen owned 21 percent of Tularik.

Receives FDA approval of Sensipar, a treatment for chronic kidney disease. Epogen patent expires.

FDA approves use of Enbrel, previously approved for rheumatoid arthritis, for chronic plaque psoriasis.

In a survey by *Science* magazine, named one of the "Top 20 Employers" among biotech and pharma companies.

2003   Epogen sales reach $2.43 billion. Spends $1.65 billion on research and development.

2002   FDA approves Neulasta—which decreases fever and infection associated with chemotherapy—and Aranesp, for treatment of leukemia associated with liver failure.

Key Financial Stats

2004 revenue: $10,550 million
1-year change: 26.3 percent

2004 global pharmaceutical sales: $10,600 million
1-year change: 35.0 percent

Personnel Highlights

Number of employees: 14,400
1-year change: 11.6 percent

ASTRAZENECA PLC

U.S. Headquarters:
1800 Concord Pike
Wilmington, DE 19850
Phone: 302-886-3000
Fax: 302-886-2972
www.astrazeneca-us.com

AstraZeneca, which is headquartered in London, focuses on developing and marketing drugs in the cardiovascular, gastrointestinal, neuroscience, oncology, respiratory and inflammation, and infection therapeutic classes. Its biggest sellers in 2004 were the acid-reflux drug Nexium, with $4.8 billion in sales; Prilosec, another acid-reflux drug, with $1.9 billion in sales; and Seroquel, an antipsychotic with $2.0 billion in sales.

The company has in recent times faced the challenge of the expiration of patents for key drugs including Prilosec, Nolvadex, and Zestril. The latter two each generated more than $1 billion in sales in 2004. The company is also looking to Crestor, a cholesterol-lowering drug, to bring in big bucks in the near future. Crestor generated more than $900 million in sales in 2004, although the company received a blow when the FDA ordered AstraZeneca to include a warning on labels that the drug may cause life-threatening muscle damage in people of Asian descent. The company received another blow when separate studies showed that Iressa, a highly touted anticancer drug, had little or no effect on life expectancy in breast and lung cancer patients.

The company's U.S. operations include the U.S. headquarters in Wilmington, Delaware; R&D facilities in Boston and Wilmington; and supply and manufacturing facilities in Newark, Delaware, and Westborough, Massachusetts. AstraZeneca employs some 11,000 people in the United States.

Recent Milestones

2005   A study by the National Cancer Institute finds that Iressa has no significant effect on breast cancer. AstraZeneca had hoped the drug would become a blockbuster.

2004   Spends $3.8 billion on drug development.

First-quarter sales of Nexium reach $935 million.

Makes *Fortune's* list of the "100 Best Companies to Work For" and *Working Mother's* list of the "100 Best Companies for Working Mothers."

In a survey by *Science* magazine, named one of the "Top 20 Employers" among biotech and pharma companies.

2003   Opens an R&D facility in India focused on developing treatments for tuberculosis.

Crestor, for high cholesterol, is approved by the FDA.

2002   FDA approves new indication for Arimidex to treat breast cancer.

Key Financial Stats

2004 revenue: $21,426 million
1-year change: 13.7 percent

2004 global pharmaceutical revenue: $21,426 million
1-year change: 13.7 percent

Personnel Highlights

Number of employees: 64,000
1-year change: 6.7 percent

BAYER CORPORATION

100 Bayer Road
Pittsburgh, PA 15205
Phone: 412-777-2000
Fax: 412-777-2034
www.bayer.com

Bayer is the pharmaceutical company next door, the name made familiar by such trusted products as Bayer Aspirin, Alka Seltzer, Bactine, Milk of Magnesia, and Flintstones Vitamins. Bayer Corporation is a wholly owned U.S. subsidiary of German company the Bayer Group and is responsible for a third of the parent company's total revenue. Bayer's business focus isn't confined to the consumer care and pharmaceutical product market: It also manufactures polymers, chemicals, diagnostics, and agriculture products.

Bayer's revenues increased in 2004 although the company's patent for Cipro expired in 2003. The antibiotic was the company's biggest seller, generating $1.6 billion in 2003. Adalat, which treats hypertension, generated about $300 million over the first half of 2004. Avelox, an antibiotic, generated more than $100 million during the same period. Sales of Levitra, an impotence drug, rose 12 percent.

Bayer has had its share of bad news in the past few years. In 2001, Bayer's profits dropped 51 percent due to a meager product pipeline. Bayer allied itself with Millennium Pharmaceuticals and CuraGen in order to regain ground. In 2002, the company had to pull its cholesterol-lowering drug Baycol from the market after it was implicated in 100 patient deaths. In mid-2005, the company paid $614 billion to settle 1,683 lawsuits.

A few years ago, insiders at Bayer suggested that bureaucracy and recent reorganizations may prove challenging to new hires.

Recent Milestones

2004   FDA approves supplemental new drug application for Avelox Tablets and I.V. for the treatment of community-acquired pneumonia caused by multidrug-resistant *Streptococcus pneumoniae*.

Named to *Working Mother*'s list of the "100 Best Companies for Working Mothers."

Bay 43-9006, which is being codeveloped by Bayer and Onyx for advanced kidney cancer, receives approval of fast-track status from the FDA.

Levitra completes its first 6 months on the market with 500,000 prescriptions filled.

In a survey by *Science* magazine, named one of the "Top 20 Employers" among biotech and pharma companies.

2003   Announces results of Levitra study, which shows that 90 percent of Levitra users report positive results.

2002   Receives FDA approval for erectile dysfunction drug Levitra, developed in partnership with GlaxoSmithKline.

Key Financial Stats

2004 revenue: $11,504 million
1-year change: 4.6 percent

2004 global pharmaceutical revenue: $5,440 million
1-year change: 1.0 percent

Personnel Highlights

Number of employees: 22,300
1-year change: –4.3 percent

BIOGEN IDEC INC.

14 Cambridge Center
Cambridge, MA 02142
Phone: 617-679-2000
Fax: 617-679-2617
www.biogenidec.com

Biogen Idec was shaken when it learned of possible side effects from Tysabri, a drug it had developed with Elan Corporation for treating multiple sclerosis. Two patients taking Tysabri died of a neurological disorder and a third was diagnosed with the same ailment. The companies asked doctors to stop administering Tysabri and ceased marketing the drug, while the companies could determine whether they could sell the drug again. But meanwhile, Biogen Idec sold the plant that was supposed to produce Tysabri to Genentech. Biogen had high hopes for Tysabri, requesting fast-track FDA approval for the drug in 2004, 1 year ahead of schedule. The company now feels a more urgent need to increase the number of products in its development pipeline and is looking to acquire late-stage drug candidates. That represents a change for the company, which was typically more strategic about acquisitions. Biogen Idec has $2.3 billion in cash for such purchases. The company continues to allocate a large portion of its budget for its 1,000 R&D employees. The company spent $687 million in R&D in 2004, about 25 percent of its revenues.

Biogen Idec resulted from a 2003 merger of Biogen and IDEC Pharmaceuticals. Biogen was founded in 1978 by a group of genetic engineering researchers—including two who would later win Nobel prizes—and before the merger it had been the number-three U.S. biotech, after Amgen and Genentech. The combined company has three drugs on the market: Avonex for multiple sclerosis, Zevalin for non-Hodgkin's lymphoma, and Amevive for chronic plaque psoriasis. Avonex is its biggest seller, with 2004 sales of $1.41 billion.

Biogen Idec also licenses products such as Schering-Plough's Intron A and hepatitis B vaccines developed by Merck. Meanwhile, it is concentrating its research on treatments for inflammatory/autoimmune diseases, neurological diseases, cancer, fibrosis, and congestive heart failure. A world-class protein manufacturer, Biogen Idec is among a handful of companies that operate bulk manufacturing facilities (in Cambridge, Massachusetts, and North Carolina's Research Triangle Park). The firm's international headquarters are in Paris.

Recent Milestones

2005   Biogen Idec suspends marketing of Tysabri, a drug for treating multiple sclerosis.

2004   In a survey by *Science* magazine, named one of the "Top 20 Employers" among biotech and pharma companies.

2003   IDEC Pharmaceuticals and Biogen merge.

        Amevive receives FDA approval.

2002   Announces collaboration with Celltech to develop and market Crohn's disease product.

        Avonex is approved for Medicare patients.

Key Financial Stats

2004 revenue: $2,212 million
1-year change: 225.6 percent

2004 global pharmaceutical revenue: $1,486 million
1-year change: 9.5 percent

Personnel Highlights

Number of employees: 4,266
1-year change: 14.5 percent

BRISTOL-MYERS SQUIBB COMPANY

345 Park Avenue
New York, NY 10154
Phone: 212-546-4000
Fax: 212-546-4020
www.bms.com

Bristol-Myers Squibb has been hit hard in recent years. Its stock price has plummeted about 60 percent since 2000. It has struggled to receive drug patents to replace drugs whose patents have expired or are soon to expire and had to cut costs and downsize its sales force. It recently paid $300 million to settle a criminal investigation by the Justice Department into alleged accounting manipulation several years ago. Squibb was even embroiled in the ImClone insider trading scandal that landed homemaking guru Martha Stewart a short prison term.

No doubt it's been a time of change at Bristol-Myers Squibb. As part of an effort to focus more on its drug development business, the firm sold Oncology Therapeutics Network, which distributes drugs to oncologists. The unit accounted for 13 percent of Squibb sales. The firm also announced it would sell the U.S. and Canadian units of its consumer products division, famed for its pain relief medications Excedrin and Bufferin (Bristol will hold onto the consumer health care division in Europe, Asia, and other regions). In mid-2005 the company also said it wouldn't advertise drugs directly to consumers until a year after FDA approval.

Yet the company is optimistic that bluer skies lie ahead. It is heartened by approval of the cancer-fighter Erbitux and is banking on a number of other drugs in its pipeline.

Bristol-Myers Squibb is a global leader in cancer treatment, and makes most of its pharmaceutical revenue in the cardiovascular and metabolic, infectious diseases (including HIV/AIDS), and psychiatric disorders therapeutic classes. Its key pharmaceuticals include the heart-attack and stroke drug Plavix ($3.32 billion in 2004 revenue) and the cholesterol-reducing drug Pravachol (which had sales of $2.63 billion in 2004). These blockbuster drugs accounted for almost one-third of the firm's revenue, although Provachol revenues declined 10 percent in 2004. Bristol-Myers Squibb's patent for the drug expires in 2006. Squibb expects to lose $1.4 billion in revenue in 2005 due to the expiration of patents. The company's patents for blockbusters Glucophage, Taxol, and BuSpar recently expired, and patents for Cefzil, an antibiotic, and Zerit, which treats HIV, will expire in 2005 and 2008, respectively. It has high hopes for Abatacept, an arthritis drug; Entecavir, a hepatitis B inhibitor; and Ixabepilone, which combats tumors.

BMS acquired a 20-percent stake in ImClone to help develop the cancer-fighting drug Erbitux. The drug received FDA approval in 2004 after being bogged down over safety concerns.

The company is at the forefront of research to improve the standard of cancer therapy drugs. It has several cytotoxics—"cell-killing" cancer drugs—in its pipeline. These next-generation drugs are designed to cause fewer side effects and treat a wider range of tumors than do traditional therapies.

In perhaps its most significant contribution to the field, Bristol teamed up with Millennium Predictive Medicines to work on a pharmacogenomic classification system for tumors. Traditionally, tumors are grouped according to the organ or tissue they originate in; in the new system, tumors will be classified by genomic makeup. This improved, scientifically precise system is more likely to indicate which tumors would respond to similar treatments.

BMS's top customers are distributors McKesson, Cardinal Health, and Amerisource-Bergen. They account for nearly 50 percent of all BMS sales.

Insiders report that the company has excellent benefits, but complain of bureaucracy.

Recent Milestones

2005   Agrees to pay $300 million to settle a criminal investigation by the Justice
        Department.

2004   Erbitux is approved by the FDA.

        Named to *Working Mother*'s list of the "100 Best Companies for Working
        Mothers."

2003   Receives FDA approval for Abilify, a promising schizophrenia drug that is the
        first new drug Bristol has had since 2000.

        Receives FDA approval for Reyataz, an HIV treatment.

2002   FDA denies approval for hypertension drug Vanlev.

Key Financial Stats

2004 revenue: $19,380 million
1-year change: –7.2 percent

2004 global pharmaceutical revenue: $15,482 million
1-year change: 4.0 percent

Personnel Highlights

Number of employees: 43,000
1-year change: –2.3 percent

CELERA GENOMICS GROUP

45 West Gude Drive
Rockville, MD 20850
Phone: 240-453-3000
Fax: 240-453-4000
www.celera.com

The Celera Genomics Group traces its roots back to 1995, when researcher Craig Venter of The Institute for Genomic Research sequenced the first complete genome of a living organism, a bacterium called *Haemophilus influenzae*. That initial discovery led Venter to develop a technique for rapidly sequencing genes, which became the basis for Celera, a company that Venter founded in 1998 along with the Applera Corporation. (Today, Celera is a business unit of Applera, along with Celera Diagnostics, which works hand-in-hand with Celera Genomics.) Since that time, Celera has made a business of selling genetic coding information and licensing the software to manage and analyze gene sequences to pharmaceutical and biotech companies.

But Celera has also restructured its business to focus on drug discovery and development. The company originally aspired to become the definitive source for genomic information by patenting gene sequences and licensing its intellectual property. However, now that the Human Genome Project has made this information available for free, that is no longer a path to riches. So the company has made developing antibody treatments in the oncology therapeutic class a goal; it is currently trying to develop treatments for pancreatic cancer.

Revenue for this company has been trending downward. In 2004, income was $60 million, down more than 30 percent from 2003. In all likelihood, Celera is looking either to partner with a bigger biotech or pharma to give it support while it tries to bring a drug to market or to be acquired by a bigger biotech or pharma for the same reason.

Recent Milestones

2005   Starts Phase I clinical trial for its Novel HDAC Inhibitor for cancer patients.

2002   Craig Venter leaves Celera to devote more time to his position as chairman at The Institute for Genomic Research. Applera Chairman Tony White assumes Venter's position temporarily.

Key Financial Stats

2004 revenue: $60 million
1-year change: −31.9 percent

Personnel Highlights

Number of employees: 530
1-year change: −29.3 percent

CHIRON CORPORATION

4560 Horton Street
Emeryville, CA 94608
Phone: 510-655-8730
Fax: 510-655-9910
www.chiron.com

Chiron was rocked by a 2004 controversy related to its Fluvirin flu vaccine: Citing violations, British authorities suspended the firm's manufacturing license at a Liverpool plant. The U.S. Justice Department and the Securities and Exchange Commission have launched their own investigations. Chiron was forced to write off its Fluvirin inventory for the third quarter of 2004—about $90 million—and didn't sell the product over the second half of the year. The drug generated about 20 percent—$219 million—of Chiron's revenue in 2003. While Chiron has subsequently received clearance to begin producing Fluvirin again, the company warned that start-up and manufacturing issues may limit production to 60 to 70 percent of its previous levels. Some competitors have taken advantage of Chiron's travails, increasing production of their own flu vaccines.

Since its inception in 1981, Chiron has evolved dramatically from a respected research institute to a highly successful commercial venture. Focusing its research on cancer and infectious disease, Chiron markets its products through three business divisions: vaccines, blood testing, and biopharmaceuticals. Chiron's vaccines division markets pediatric vaccines ($201 million in revenue in 2004), flu vaccines ($153 million), and travel vaccines ($97 million). Chiron also earns revenue from several pharma companies that use Chiron technologies in their drugs. Its blood-testing segment mostly produces immunodiagnostic tests for the detection of hepatitis viruses and retroviruses and instruments systems to automate testing and data collection. Among the company's biopharmaceutical products, TOBI ($212 million in 2004), used to treat cystic fibrosis, is its most important. Proleukin, a treatment for renal cancer and melanoma, and the Betaseron multiple sclerosis drug are also big earners. Chiron established its research and development reputation early in its history, creating the first engineered vaccines (for hepatitis B and pertussis, a.k.a., whooping cough) and mapping the HIV genome.

Alliances and acquisitions have been key to Chiron's success—Novartis and Chiron share technologies (indeed, Novartis owns 42 percent of Chiron), and among Chiron's acquisitions are Proleukin's manufacturer, Cetus; PathoGenesis Corp., a developer of antibiotics; Matrix Pharmaceutical, a developer of cancer drugs; and PowderJect Pharmaceuticals, which has beefed up Chiron's vaccine offerings. Fluvirin became part of its stable when Chiron acquired PowderJect. In order to focus on the commercial side of the business, Chiron sold off its quality control, electrophoresis, and vision divisions.

Insiders report that the entrepreneurial spirit is alive and well at Chiron—and that instead of a feeling of competition between scientists, there is a contagious, team-oriented drive to discover.

Recent Milestones

2005   Announces it will produce 18 to 26 million doses of Fluvirin, fewer than expected.

2004   Begins collaborating with XOMA to develop cancer drugs.

In a survey by *Science* magazine, named one of the "Top 20 Employers" among biotech and pharma companies.

2003   Acquires British vaccine maker PowderJect Pharmaceuticals.

Creates a test to screen blood for West Nile virus.

2002   Acquires Matrix Pharmaceutical, increasing its presence in the cancer therapeutics market.

Key Financial Stats

2004 revenue: $1,723 billion
1-year change: −2.4 percent

Personnel Highlights

Number of employees: 5,400
1-year change: 1.3 percent

ELI LILLY AND COMPANY

Lilly Corporate Center
Indianapolis, IN 46285
Phone: 317-276-2000
Fax: 317-277-6579
www.lilly.com

Eli Lilly is a pioneer in pharmaceutical research and the treatment of disease. Among its many coups, Lilly lays claim to developing the first commercial insulin product in 1923; creating the first human health care product—insulin—using recombinant DNA technology; and introducing Prozac, the first major drug in the selective serotonin-reuptake inhibitor class of antidepressants. Lilly has hundreds of manufacturing and R&D alliances around the world. About half of Lilly's 44,500 employees work in the United States. About 8,400 employees, almost a quarter of the workforce, work in R&D and focus primarily on neuroscience, endocrinology, infectious disease, oncology, and cardiovascular disease. Lilly traditionally benefits from a strong pipeline.

Lilly's future seems more secure than that of many of its competitors, thanks to its stable of big-market products. The company currently has four $1-billion-plus blockbusters: Zyprexa (2004 sales of $4.4 billion), a treatment for schizophrenia and bipolar disorder; pancreatic cancer drug Gemzar; insulin drug Humalog; and Evista. Such achievements have, among other things, made possible the development of a new R&D facility and insulin manufacturing plant in Indianapolis, where Lilly is headquartered.

The company has not been without its problems. In June 2005 Lilly announced that it would settle most of its liability claims related to Zyprexa. The lawsuits alleged that the company didn't adequately display warnings that the drug could increase the risk of hyperglycemia and diabetes. Lilly said it would establish a $690 million fund to cover about 8,000 lawsuits filed before September 2003.

Recent Milestones

2005   Declares a dividend of $0.38 for its third quarter, the third consecutive quarter in which it had declared a $0.38 dividend.

Makes *Fortune*'s list of the "100 Best Companies to Work For."

2004   Cialis launches during the Super Bowl; football coach and all-around tough guy Mike Ditka is its spokesman.

Named to *Working Mother*'s list of the "100 Best Companies for Working Mothers."

In a survey by *Science* magazine, named one of the "Top 20 Employers" among biotech and pharma companies.

2003   Ranks first among pharma companies in providing discount-priced drugs to patients who cannot afford to use them at full price.

FDA approves Cialis, for erectile dysfunction, and Symbyax, for bipolar depression.

2002   Receives FDA approval for Strattera, for the treatment of ADHD, and Forteo, for osteoporosis.

Key Financial Stats

2004 revenue: $13,858 million
1-year change: 10.1 percent

2004 global pharmaceutical revenue: $13,059 million
1-year change: 4.0 percent

Personnel Highlights

Number of employees: 44,500
1-year change: –3.5 percent

GENENTECH, INC.

1 DNA Way
South San Francisco, CA 94080
Phone: 650-225-1000
Fax: 650-225-6000
www.gene.com

Genentech, the oldest of all the biotech companies, was founded in 1976. Because it has a strong focus on R&D, it has achieved top honors in this category—Genentech's scientists are in the top 1 percent for total worldwide citations received in scientific journals. Its research focuses on oncology, cardiovascular disease, and immunological disease. The company is majority owned by the Big Pharma giant Roche.

Genentech's dedication to R&D has resulted in a healthy product portfolio. The company has 13 protein-based products on the market and some 20 more in the pipeline. (Among its credits, Genentech was the first biotech company to successfully scale up protein manufacturing from small research quantities to the amounts needed for clinical trials and marketing.) In 2004, its biggest selling drug was Rituxan, a lymphoma treatment developed with IDEC Pharmaceuticals, with $1.7 billion in sales. Tarceva, which treats lung cancer, generated $56 million in the last 2 months of 2004 after gaining FDA approval in November.

In an effort to increase the velocity with which it creates new revenue streams, Genentech has taken to testing drug combinations before they have been approved for the public by the FDA. The potential upside of this tactic is rapidly rising revenues, but the risk is that Genentech ends up wasting money on drug-combination tests if any of the component drugs in the combination are not approved by the FDA.

Insiders say that Genentech is very team-oriented and frowns on office politics.

Recent Milestones

2005   Makes *Fortune*'s list of the "100 Best Companies to Work For."

2004   Avastin is approved by the FDA, and the drug goes to market.

Named to *Working Mother*'s list of the "100 Best Companies for Working Mothers."

In a survey by *Science* magazine, named one of the "Top 20 Employers" among biotech and pharma companies.

2003   Avastin, for colorectal cancer, receives fast-track development approval from the FDA.

2003   Raptiva, a psoriasis drug developed with XOMA, and Xolair, for adolescent and adult asthma, launch.

2002   Genentech ordered to give $300 million in unpaid royalties to City of Hope for two of its scientists' work in the development of Humulin.

Key Financial Stats

2004 revenue: $3,980 million
1-year change: 42.2 percent

2004 global pharmaceutical revenue: $3,749 million
1-year change: 43.0 percent

Personnel Highlights

Number of employees: 7,646
1-year change: 22.8 percent

GENZYME CORPORATION

500 Kendall Street
Cambridge, MA 02142
Phone: 617-252-7500
Fax: 617-252-7600
www.genzyme.com

Genzyme's scientists put the company on the map when they realized its first important success in 1992: Through collaborative gene research with the University of Iowa, the company rolled out breakthrough treatments for cystic fibrosis. Building on this research, in 2000, the company produced a cystic fibrosis test, the most comprehensive one to hit the market.

Of course, some would say that 1998 marked the turning point for Genzyme, when it streamlined its therapeutics development by closing its chemicals business and spinning off its research products division. By doing so, it was able to focus its business and specialize in its strong suits: the areas of genetic disease, renal disease, and osteoarthritis. That year was a big one for Genzyme: It won FDA approval for Renagel, a phosphate binder for kidney disease, and for cancer-screening agent Thyrogen, created in partnership with Knoll Pharmaceuticals. A year later, Genzyme Transgenics, of which Genzyme owns a 25 percent stake, began experimenting with goat cloning in an effort to introduce a human gene responsible for making anticoagulants. This ambitious research is aimed at developing such breakthrough treatments as a new malaria vaccine, therapies for HIV, and a diabetes vaccine.

The company has recently expanded through acquisitions. In 2005 it acquired Bone Care International, which developed vitamin D hormones for treating secondary hyperparathyroidism. In 2004 it acquired ILEX Oncology, which produces a drug for pediatric leukemia.

Genzyme's efforts focus on six major areas: lysosomal storage disorders, renal disease, orthopedics, transplant and immune diseases, oncology, and genetics/diagnostics.

Genzyme's biggest money-maker is Cerezyme, a pricey drug for patients with Gaucher disease; in 2004, Cerezyme generated $839 million in revenue, up $100 million over 2003. Renagel, a treatment for end-stage renal disease, generated $364 million in revenue for Genzyme in 2004.

Among the most promising drugs in development for Genzyme are Myozyme for treating Pompe disease, a debilitating muscle ailment, and Clofarabine for treating leukemia and solid tumors.

Insiders say the company does a good job of emphasizing teamwork and collaboration.

Recent Milestones

2005   Announces that second quarter 2005 revenue increased 22 percent to $668 million.

2004   Forms joint venture with medical-devices maker Medtronic to target cardiac repair 2003

       Sells its cardiothoracic-devices business to Teleflex.

       Acquires SangStat Medical Corporation, a biotech focused on immunology.

       Fabryzyme, for Fabry disease, and Aldurazyme, a drug developed with BioMarin Pharmaceutical for Hurler syndrome, are approved by the FDA.

2002   Acquires Peptimmune, which develops immunology therapies for autoimmune and allergic disease.

Key Financial Stats

2004 revenue: $2,201 million
1-year change: 28.4 percent

2004 global pharmaceutical revenue: $1,976 million
1-year change: 34.0 percent

Personnel Highlights

Number of employees: 7,100
1-year change: 26.2 percent

GILEAD SCIENCES, INC.

333 Lakeside Drive
Foster City, CA 94404
Phone: 650-574-3000
Fax: 650-578-9264
www.gilead.com

Gilead Sciences, which until 2001 had the current U.S. Secretary of Defense Donald Rumsfeld as its chairman of the board, researches and develops treatments for cancer and infectious diseases such as the flu, HIV, and HIV-related infections. The company is on a roll, as it has had three drugs approved in the past few years. Viread, an HIV drug, is the company's biggest seller, accounting for some 40 percent of overall revenue; it generated $783 million in revenue in 2004. AmBisome, which the company gained when it acquired NexStar Pharmaceuticals in 1999, is Gilead's second biggest seller, generating $212 million in sales in 2004. AmBisome treats HIV-related systemic fungal infections, including aspergillosis, candidiasis, and *Cryptococcus* infections. Other products include Hepsera and the flu treatment Tamiflu.

Although Gilead sold several cancer therapy products it was developing to OSI Pharmaceuticals a few years ago, the company had a number of promising drugs in its pipeline, particularly treatments for hepatitis B and HIV. Emtriva, an HIV drug, received FDA approval in 2003. Hepsera, a drug that treats hepatitis B, received European Union marketing approval in 2003.

Gilead is focused on drug development. It spent $224 million on R&D in 2004. Other companies market its drugs, and Gilead has marketing alliances with major players in the drug industry, such as Pfizer and Hoffmann-La Roche.

Insiders report that Gilead, perhaps due to its small size, is a friendly place.

Recent Milestones

2005   Announces second quarter revenues of $495 million, up 55 percent over the second quarter of 2004.

2004   Enters joint venture with Bristol-Myers Squibb to develop HIV treatment.

2003   Emtriva, for HIV, receives FDA marketing approval.

Acquires Triangle Pharmaceuticals, which focuses on developing antiviral medications.

2002   Hepsera is approved by the FDA.

Turns an annual profit for the first time.

Key Financial Stats

2004 revenue: $1,325 million
1-year change: 52.6 percent

Personnel Highlights

Number of employees: 1,654
1-year change: 16.1 percent

GLAXOSMITHKLINE PLC

U.S. Headquarters:
1 Franklin Plaza
Philadelphia, PA 19101
Phone: 888-825-5249
Fax: 215-751-3233
www.gsk.com

The days when GlaxoSmithKline was the world's largest manufacturer of pharmaceuticals are gone. The company now ranks second, behind Pfizer. Growth has been slower for the company than for some of its competitors—just 2 percent for its pharmaceutical products. Still, the European pharmaceutical behemoth has an array of key drugs in some of the most profitable markets: anti-infectives, central nervous system and respiratory therapeutics, and medicines for gastrointestinal and metabolic conditions.

GlaxoSmithKline's current challenges include generic competition for a number of its drugs that are no longer under patent protection. Its over-the-counter ulcer treatment, Zantac, was the world's best-selling prescription drug before the patent expired in 1997 and Novopharm began producing it. And the company recently lost patent protection for antidepressants Paxil and Wellbutrin, though some formulations remain protected.

But there's a lot to look forward to at GlaxoSmithKline. For one thing, it has 140 drugs in the clinical stage of development, with a number of potential blockbusters; GlaxoSmithKline spent $5.1 billion on R&D in 2004. For another thing, it has several blockbuster drugs. Seretide/Advair, an asthma treatment, had $4.4 billion in sales in 2004—about 12 percent of the company's overall sales. Avandia generated $2.0 billion in sales in 2004. In 2004 GlaxoSmithKline arranged with Watson Pharmaceuticals to distribute a generic version of Wellbutrin. Other GlaxoSmithKline blockbusters include the antiviral medications Combivir and Valtrex.

Insiders report that the company is still feeling growing pains from the 2001 SmithKline Beecham merger: "There's bitterness among the old SKB employees, a little bit of 'back before the merger' kind of talk," one says. "This is such a big company that people tend to stick with their department, their immediate coworkers."

Recent Milestones

2005   Works out an exchange of licenses with Merck for a human papillomavirus vaccine. If Merck brings the drug to market, GSK will receive royalties.

2004   New York Attorney General Eliot Spitzer sues GlaxoSmithKline for allegedly withholding negative information about its antidepressant Paxil in treating children and teens. FDA claims that Paxil advertisement deceptively targets consumers by pursuing people with everyday worries and uses background music and "attention-grabbing visuals" to distract from possible risks from the drug. Two months after the suit is filed, GSK becomes the first major drug manufacturer to agree to publicly disclose information about its clinical trials.

In a survey by *Science* magazine, named one of the "Top 20 Employers" among biotech and pharma companies.

Named to *Working Mother*'s list of the "100 Best Companies for Working Mothers."

2003   FDA extends review period for Bexxar, a drug for non-Hodgkin's lymphoma.

2002   Receives FDA approval for Levitra, developed in partnership with Bayer.

Key Financial Stats

2004 revenue: $39,032 million
1-year change: 2.1 percent

2004 global pharmaceutical revenue: $31,377 million
1-year change: 5.0 percent

Personnel Highlights

Number of employees: 100,019
1-year change: –0.9 percent

JOHNSON & JOHNSON

1 Johnson & Johnson Plaza
New Brunswick, NJ 08933
Phone: 732-524-0400
Fax: 732-524-3300
www.jnj.com

Johnson & Johnson is the world's largest manufacturer of health-care products and one of the most diversified product makers. In addition to making and marketing prescription drugs, the company does business in consumer pharmaceuticals (including familiar brands Tylenol, Motrin, Reach, and Band-Aid) and medical devices and diagnostics (Acuvue contact lenses, surgical instruments, joint replacements, orthopedic products, and sutures). Its biggest selling pharmaceutical in 2004 was Procrit, which accounted for 8 percent—about $3.6 billion—of the company's overall sales. Procrit stimulates red blood cell production in cancer patients who develop anemia as a result of chemotherapy. Risperdal, for schizophrenia, generated about $3.1 billion for J&J in 2004.

J&J has been active on the acquisition front. In mid-2005, it purchased Peninsula Pharmaceuticals, which produces the antibiotic doripenem. Doripenem is in the last stage of clinical trials. Earlier in the year it announced plans to acquire Guidant in a deal worth $24 billion. Guidant manufactures cardiovascular therapeutic devices.

The company's broad product base is a result of its unique organizational structure, which consists of affiliates and operating arms around the world. Its strategy is to acquire and ally itself with companies that develop new technologies—J&J acquired Procrit and Risperdal.

J&J has an enormous R&D department. It spent $5.2 billion in 2004 on R&D, an increase of more than $500 million.

Insiders report that J&J does a good job of giving employees real responsibility and helping employees design their career paths. With minorities accounting for nearly a third of its staff, the company also has a good diversity record. Its careers website and other recruiting practices regularly win kudos from experts.

Recent Milestones

2005   Completes acquisition of Peninsula Pharmaceuticals.

2004   Veridex, a Johnson & Johnson company formed in 2004, announces plans for a fall 2004 launch of the CellSearch System, a new cancer diagnostic technology.

Named to *Working Mother*'s list of the "100 Best Companies for Working Mothers."

In a survey by *Science* magazine, named one of the "Top 20 Employers" among biotech and pharma companies.

2003   Risperdal Consta is approved for schizophrenia.

Acquires Scios, a biopharma firm focused on cardiovascular and anti-inflammatory drug development; Orquest, a biotech focused on orthopedics and spinal injuries; 3-Dimensional Pharmaceuticals, which has a technology platform that aids in the discovery and development of therapeutic small molecules; and OraPharma, a specialty pharma focused on oral therapeutics.

Key Financial Stats

2004 revenue: $47,348 million
1-year change: 13.1 percent

2004 global pharmaceutical revenue: $22,128 million
1-year change: 13.0 percent

Personnel Highlights

Number of employees: 109,900
1-year change: –0.6 percent

MERCK & CO., INC.

1 Merck Drive
Whitehouse Station, NJ 08889
Phone: 908-423-1000
Fax: 908-735-1253
www.merck.com

Most Merck headlines in 2004 and 2005 haven't been the sort it craves. The first of some 4,000 lawsuits alleging that the company marketed the blockbuster drug Vioxx despite evidence that it was unsafe were filed in July 2005. Vioxx generated $2.5 billion in revenue in 2003 and $1.4 billion in 2004 before Merck pulled the drug off market in September. Merck's action came after a more recent study showed that it increased the risk of heart disease. More than 20 million people have taken Vioxx, according to news reports. Merck has maintained that Vioxx didn't lead to heart problems and allocated nearly $700 million to fight the cases. But the cost of litigation may be less of a problem than the blow to Merck's reputation. A lawyer representing the widow in the first case tried to paint Merck as a greedy and dishonest company. Merck's attorneys denied this characterization, pointing to FDA letters that were part of Vioxx's approval process.

Net income dropped almost 15 percent in 2004 following several lackluster years. The firm has struggled to produce blockbuster drugs over this period.

Still, Merck is sure to remain among the world's largest and oldest pharmaceutical companies, fiercely independent about its methods and a major supplier of important products. Unlike its larger competitors, who mostly license drugs from other companies, Merck tries to develop products at its own laboratories. Similarly, it likes to do its own research. Merck spends just 5 percent of its research budget outside the company, whereas other pharmaceutical firms outsource up to 80 percent of their research. It spent more than $4 billion on R&D in 2004. In addition, it didn't pursue mergers and acquisitions as did some of its larger competitors.

One of Merck's more dramatic recent successes was Crixivan, an HIV drug introduced in 1996. After 18 months on the market, the protease inhibitor cut AIDS-related deaths by 60 percent; and when used with two other HIV drugs, Crixivan significantly reduces the spread of the infection.

Currently, Merck's biggest seller is Zocor, the cholesterol treatment, which had sales of $5.2 billion in 2004, an increase of $500 million over 2003. But a 2006 patent expiration date for Zocor could be bad news for Merck, which has already seen patents for such successful drugs as Vasotec, Pepcid, Prinivil, and Prilosec expire over the past 5 years.

Drugs that contributed to Merck's 2004 sales growth included Fosamax for osteoporosis ($3.2 billion), Cozaar/Hyzaar for high blood pressure ($2.8 million), and Singulair for asthma and seasonal allergic rhinitis ($2.1 billion).

Yet it may not have any near-term blockbusters in development. Analysts have said that Merck's reluctance to rely on the licensing agreements so prevalent in the industry may be hurting the company, since the drug development process is so long and risky.

However, Merck has some very promising drugs in earlier stages, so in the longer term its pipeline appears to be in good shape. The company has taken to using DNA chips to weed out drugs that are bound to fail when they reach human trials; it's hoping to increase the efficiency of its R&D process in developing saleable drugs as a result.

Insiders say that the bureaucracy at Merck can sometimes be challenging.

Recent Milestones

2005   Announces that it will provide discounts on many of its prescription medicines to uninsured Americans.

Receives approval for Fosamax Plus D, which combines Foxamax with vitamin D into one tablet. Learns that its patent for Fosamax, which treats osteoporosis, will expire 10 years sooner than it expected.

FDA clears Merck to sell Vioxx, its arthritis pain medication.

2004   Announces plans with Bristol-Myers Squibb and Gilead Sciences to develop a fixed-dose combination of three HIV medicines.

Named to *Working Mother*'s list of the "100 Best Companies for Working Mothers."

In a survey by *Science* magazine, named one of the "Top 20 Employers" among biotech and pharma companies.

2003   Acquires Banyu Pharmaceutical of Japan.

FDA approves Cancidas, an antifungal medication, and Emend, an antiemetic for chemotherapy patients.

2002   Signs technology license agreement with Celera Genomics to access its human and mouse genome databases.

FDA approves new use of Vioxx for rheumatoid arthritis.

Key Financial Stats

2004 revenue: $22,938 million
1-year change: 2.0 percent

2004 global pharmaceutical revenue: $21,493 million
1-year change: –4.0 percent

Personnel Highlights

Number of employees: 63,000
1-year change: 104.4 percent

NOVARTIS AG

U.S. Headquarters:
608 Fifth Avenue
New York, NY 10020
Phone: 212-307-1122
Fax: 212-246-0185
www.novartis.com

Novartis has been having an active 2005. While continuing to pursue research and product development in its typically aggressive manner, it announced that it was purchasing Hexal of Germany and Eon Labs for $8.4 billion and the over-the-counter unit of Bristol-Myers Squibb for $660 million. The former acquisition will make Novartis the world's largest generic drug company.

Novartis, which means "new skills," is the sizable offspring of a 1996 merger that combined two Swiss pharmaceutical giants, Sandoz and Ciba. Since then, CEO Daniel Vasella has taken the company to new heights by incorporating ideas about drug development that he pioneered while running Sandoz. Drug development used to be thought of as a linear process that went from research to development to marketing. Vasella realized that better integration of these three phases would drastically increase efficiency. The company built a reputation for developing drugs more quickly than other companies in its industry. While a European-based company, the largest share of its pharmaceutical revenue comes from the United States.

The company focuses on the following areas: cardiovascular/metabolism/endocrinology, oncology/hematology, central nervous system, transplantation/immunology, respiratory/dermatology, rheumatology/bone/hormone-replacement therapy/gastrointestinal, and ophthalmics. Its biggest sellers in 2004 were hypertension drug Diovan ($3.1 billion), tumor inhibitor Gleevec ($1.6 billion), and Zometa ($1.1 billion) for cancer complications.

In May 2002, Novartis established a new hub for its research operations in Cambridge, Massachusetts. The company overhauled a 500,000-square-foot building that belonged to the New England Confectionary Company. Novartis uses the state-of-the-art center for R&D related to diabetes, cardiovascular disease, and infectious diseases. In 2004 the company spent $4.2 billion on R&D.

Novartis owns some 20 percent of rival drugmaker Roche.

Recent Milestones

2005   Announces deal to purchase Hexal and Eon Labs.

Net sales for first 6 months rise 11 percent to $15.1 billion. Net income rises 12 percent to $3.1 billion.

FDA requires Novartis to place extra warnings on its epilepsy drug Trileptal, after several patients taking it developed serious skin ailments.

2004   Sandoz, a Novartis company, acquires Canadian generic injectables maker Sabex Holdings.

Named to *Working Mother*'s list of the "100 Best Companies for Working Mothers."

In a survey by *Science* magazine, named one of the "Top 20 Employers" among biotech and pharma companies.

2003   Acquires Idenix Pharmaceuticals, a biopharma company focused on drugs for viral and other infectious diseases, and Enablex, an incontinence drug, from Pfizer.

Settles legal battle with GlaxoSmithKline, agreeing to pay a royalty on any revenue from its sales of generic versions of Glaxo's patented antibiotic Augmentin.

FDA approves Xolair, an asthma drug developed by Novartis along with Genentech and Tanox. The drug has also been approved for sale in Australia. Also receives record-fast FDA approval for the blood cancer drug Gleevec, based on early-stage data.

Key Financial Stats

2004 revenue: $28,247 million
1-year change: 13.6 percent

2004 global pharmaceutical revenue: $18,497 million
1-year change: 2.5 percent

Personnel Highlights

Number of employees: 81,392
1-year change: 3.6 percent

PFIZER INC

235 East 42nd Street
New York, NY 10017
Phone: 212-573-2323
Fax: 212-573-7851
www.pfizer.com

Like Merck's Vioxx troubles, Pfizer has faced its own controversy regarding top COX-2 inhibitor drugs. In late 2004, it announced that Celebrex, which generated $3.3 billion in sales, could increase the risk of heart attack and pulled its TV and radio ads. In April 2005, the FDA ordered Pfizer to stop selling Bextra, another COX-2 inhibitor. The same month, at the request of European regulators, Pfizer pulled the drug from the European Union market. The company had placed a warning on Bextra packaging that it could increase the risk of strokes, clots, and heart attacks. Meanwhile, the FDA is also investigating whether Viagra is associated with blindness due to ischemic injury to the optic nerve.

With its 2003 purchase of Pharmacia, Pfizer became the biggest of Big Pharma. The merger added a number of big drugs to Pfizer's portfolio, including Celebrex, Genotropin (human growth hormone replacement therapy), and Zyvox (an antibiotic). But Pfizer also knows how to develop drugs in-house. Indeed, the company spends more money every year on R&D (a whopping $7.7 billion in 2004) than any of its Big Pharma peers. The result of this dual-pronged approach: more blockbuster sellers than any other pharmaceutical company (Lipitor, Norvasc, and Zoloft, among them).

Probably its best-known drug is the impotency treatment Viagra, launched in 1998, which earned a record-breaking $100 million in its first month and sold faster than any other new drug to hit the market. Viagra's sales in 2004 were $1.6 billion. Yet that's dwarfed by sales of other drugs in a variety of areas. Its cholesterol-fighting drug Lipitor generated $10.9 billion alone in 2004, while Norvasc generated $4.5 billion, and Zoloft generated $3.4 billion.

In addition to pharmaceuticals, which make up about 90 percent of the company's revenues, Pfizer develops over-the-counter brands, including Visine, BenGay, Sudafed, and Zantac. It also boasts an animal-health division, which makes antiparasitic medicines and vaccines for livestock, and a capsule-manufacturing business. A few years ago, in order to concentrate on pharmaceuticals, Pfizer sold its Tetra fish-care products business, its Adams confectionary products business, its Schick-Wilkinson shaving products business, and several of its women's health-care product lines. It also divested the Pharmacia Diagnostics business.

Pfizer's recruiting operations are highly regarded in the field of HR. It also regularly wins kudos as an employee-friendly company.

Recent Milestones

2005   Named to *Fortune's* list of the "100 Best Companies to Work For."

2004   Acquires Esperion Therapeutics, a biopharma company focused on the development of high-density lipoprotein–targeted (good cholesterol) therapies for the treatment of cardiovascular disease.

Sells its *in vitro* allergy and autoimmune diagnostic testing business, acquired as part of the Pharmacia deal, to private equity investors.

Warner-Lambert, a subsidiary of Pfizer, pleads guilty to criminal health-care fraud charges relating to its misbranding of Neurontin by failing to provide adequate directions for use and by introduction into interstate commerce of an unapproved new drug.

Named to *Working Mother's* list of the "100 Best Companies for Working Mothers."

In a survey by *Science* magazine, named one of the "Top 20 Employers" among biotech and pharma companies.

2003   Acquires Pharmacia for $54 billion.

2002   Agrees to collaborate with Eisai to promote anticonvulsant drug Cerebyx.

Arthritis medication Celebrex reaches $3 billion in sales.

Inspra, a blood pressure medication, is approved by the FDA.

Key Financial Stats

2004 revenue: $52,516 million

1-year change: 16.2 percent

2004 global pharmaceutical revenue: $46,133 million

1-year change: 16.0 percent

Personnel Highlights

Number of employees: 115,000

1-year change: −5.7 percent

ROCHE HOLDING

U.S. Headquarters:
340 Kingsland Street
Nutley, NJ 07110
Phone: 973-235-5000
Fax: 973-235-7605
www.roche.com

Roche, which is 20 percent owned by Novartis, began in 1896 as a medical supply company in Basel, Switzerland. In the '50s and '60s, Roche attained its leadership position in chemotherapy with Fluorouracil Roche. In 1963, it launched the still-popular benzodiazepine tranquilizer Valium. Roche's most successful product, the antibiotic Rocephin, was introduced in 1982, outselling all other Roche products by 1987. In recent years, Roche has continued to focus on the development of cancer therapeutics as well as treatments for rheumatoid arthritis, AIDS and other infectious diseases, and central nervous system disorders. Hepatitis B and C treatment Pegasys is approved in the United States. Roche is also licensing Fuzeon, the most clinically advanced in a new class of AIDS treatments, from Trimeris.

Roche has six drugs that generated $1 billion or more in 2004. Its top seller was Rituxan, a treatment for non-Hodgkin's lymphoma, with sales of nearly $4.2 billion. Epogin, a treatment for anemia, had sales of $1.6 billion. Pegasys had sales of more than $1.2 billion. Herceptin, a cancer treatment; CellCept, a drug used for transplant patients; and Rocephin, a treatment for bacterial infections, all generated at least $1 billion apiece. Avastin, a relatively new product for treating cancer, had sales of $690 million.

Thanks to heavy R&D spending ($4.5 billion in 2004), Roche's pipeline is brimming with various developments. This is due in part to its 2001 acquisition of Japanese pharmaceutical company Chugai, which specialized in the development of therapeutics for central nervous system, respiratory, gastrointestinal, and metabolic disorders.

In addition, Roche's fat pipeline can be attributed to its expansion into the diagnostics market, focusing primarily on genomics, blood screening, and virology. Roche is one of several biopharmaceutical companies trying to gain a stake in this growing field. Roche's source for genomics information—genetic factors linked to diseases—is Icelandic genetic firm deCODE, with which it made an R&D alliance. Roche also owns some 60 percent of Genentech.

On the downside, Roche is facing legal battles due to side effects of its Accutane acne drug, which include birth defects and suicidal behavior.

Insiders say that the company has a real team environment and rave about the compensation and benefits.

Recent Milestones

2005   Named to *Fortune's* list of the "100 Best Companies to Work For."

2004   Roche gains approval for and/or launches nine drugs.

In a survey by *Science* magazine, named one of the "Top 20 Employers" among biotech and pharma companies.

2003   Sells vitamins and fine chemicals business.

2002   Enters into 3-year alliance with deCODE, an Icelandic genetic firm, to research and develop therapeutics for four undisclosed diseases.

Key Financial Stats

2004 revenue: $27,630 million
1-year change: 9.9 percent

2004 global pharmaceutical revenue: $17,322 million
1-year change: 41.5 percent

Personnel Highlights

Number of employees: 64,703
1-year change: −1.0 percent

SCHERING-PLOUGH CORPORATION

2000 Galloping Hill Road
Kenilworth, NJ 07033
Phone: 908-298-4000
Fax: 908-298-7653
www.sch-plough.com

Schering-Plough rode a wave of double-digit growth through the '80s and '90s with breakthrough developments, from antihistamines and corticosteroids to antibiotics, anti-infectives, and antiviral products. The company is highly diversified: Among the products it develops and markets are prescription drugs, animal health-care treatments, over-the-counter drugs (e.g., Afrin and Nasonex), foot-care products (e.g., Dr. Scholl's), and skin-care products (e.g., Coppertone and Bain de Soleil).

But the company's performance has been sluggish. Revenues sagged in 2004 as some of its blockbuster drugs lost steam, including its allergy medication Claritin. Revenues from Claritin dropped after it stopped being a prescription drug. Sales of its hepatitis drugs Intron A, PEG-Intron, and Rebetol also sank. Schering-Plough's best-sellers are Remicade, which generated $746 million in 2004, and allergy medications Clarinex and Nasonex, which generated $692 million and $594 million, respectively, in 2004.

The company's drug pipeline is weaker than many of its competitors. To generate revenue, Schering-Plough worked with Merck to develop cholesterol drug Zetia. It has research agreements with Valeant Pharmaceuticals and ALZA.

Schering-Plough was the subject of merger rumors in 2003 with Merck as the potential acquirer of the company, but Merck decided against the transaction. In response to hard times resulting from the decline of Claritin, the company is looking to cut costs via measures such as cutting dividends and employee raises and bonuses, as well as offering early retirement to employees.

Recent Milestones

2005   Acquires the assets of NeoGenesis Pharmaceuticals, which creates tools to help researchers identify new drug candidates.

2004   Settles SEC charges that its Polish arm bribed government officials and failed to report those bribes, paying $500,000.

Named to *Working Mother*'s list of the "100 Best Companies for Working Mothers."

In a survey by *Science* magazine, named one of the "Top 20 Employers" among biotech and pharma companies.

2003   Hires a number of Pharmacia executives after that company is absorbed by Pfizer.

Key Financial Stats

2004 revenue: $8,272 million
1-year change: −0.7 percent

2004 global pharmaceutical revenue: $6,417 million
1-year change: 4.0 percent

Personnel Highlights

Number of employees: 30,500
1-year change: 0 percent

WYETH

5 Giralda Farms
Madison, NJ 07940
Phone: 973-660-5000
Fax: 973-660-7026
www.wyeth.com

Wyeth has been around since the 1860s, but the former drugstore has since morphed into a research laboratory and finally a pharmaceutical and household products giant that swallows up or joins forces with a diverse range of developers and manufacturers as a means to diversify and broaden its product range—a strategy that's been in place since the 1940s. In 1943, Wyeth—known as American Home Products until March 2002—acquired six companies, which turned out, among other things, household goods, food, and medical supplies.

It's only been in the last 10 years or so that the company has begun to really focus on four major divisions: the prescription pharmaceuticals and vaccines division, which now earns Wyeth some 80 percent of its revenues; its R&D arm; over-the-counter products (e.g., Advil, Centrum, Dimetapp, Preparation H); and animal-health and veterinary medicine.

The company's biggest seller is antidepressant Effexor, which generated more than $3.3 billion in 2004—about 20 percent of Wyeth's revenue. Protonix, a treatment for acid reflux, accounted for nearly $1.6 billion in revenue, while vaccine Prevnar pulled in almost $1.1 billion.

Recent Milestones

2005   Announces plans to reduce its sales force by as much as 30 percent by the end of the year.

2004   Named to *Working Mother*'s list of the "100 Best Companies for Working Mothers."

In a survey by *Science* magazine, named one of the "Top 20 Employers" among biotech and pharma companies.

2003   FDA approves Effexor, an anxiety medication. FluMist is approved and launched in the United States.

Premarin sales drop 32 percent following NIH clinical trials.

2002   Changes name to Wyeth, after its ancestor, the Philadelphia drugstore John Wyeth and Brother, which opened in 1860.

Key Financial Stats

2004 revenue: $17,358 million
1-year change: 9.5 percent

2004 global pharmaceutical revenue: $13,964 million
1-year change: 10.5 percent

Personnel Highlights

Number of employees: 51,401
1-year change: −1.9 percent

On the Job

Science Jobs

Engineering Jobs

Sales Jobs

Other Specialties

Real People Profiles

Science Jobs

The entry-level job title in most pharmaceutical and biotech companies is lab technician. The work can be somewhat tedious, but a lab tech position can be an excellent way into the industry.

If you've got a BS or MS degree with previous lab experience, either in school or in industry, you can generally find work as a research associate. Research associates do real science, conducting experiments and analyzing data under the close supervision of more senior scientists. Research associates often have a number after their title (e.g., Research Associate II) to indicate seniority level. Above the research associate is the research specialist (this title varies somewhat—it's sometimes called pharmaceuticals specialist, among other things), who generally has more autonomy and creative input into his or her research than the associate does.

PhDs who have completed their postdocs typically enter as associate scientists. In rare instances, research specialists (without PhDs) are promoted to this level. Associate scientists have considerable autonomy over their own research, though they work in fairly close collaboration with a supervisor. The step after associate scientist is scientist—a position that requires running the lab and planning and executing large-scale research projects. Above the scientist is the senior scientist, who oversees the work of several scientists but no longer works in the lab. Scientists at all levels have the option of leaving the science track for management-track positions. Insiders say that for employees who don't have PhDs (and who don't intend to go back to school to get one), the management track holds many more opportunities for promotion than the non-PhD science track.

LAB TECH

Lab techs perform the routine maintenance tasks—cleaning and maintaining glassware, working with animal colonies, operating lab equipment, and so on—that are needed to keep labs functioning. A high school diploma is required, and many people with college degrees start here as well.

Salary range: $27,000 to $35,000

RESEARCH ASSOCIATE

A BS or MS in some form of chemistry or biology and experience working in a lab are typically required to land this job. Associates work at the bench, conducting experiments under the guidance of PhD scientists. If you're coming out of school with some lab experience but no PhD and you want to work in R&D, this is the job for you.

Salary range: $40,000 to $71,000

RESEARCH SCIENTIST

After receiving a PhD and completing a postdoc, a scientist can get a job as a research scientist (sometimes the initial title is Associate Scientist), designing and conducting experiments and writing up results for publication when appropriate.

Salary range: $65,000 to $110,000

QUALITY CONTROL ANALYST

QC analysts are responsible for the biological and chemical evaluation of products, materials, and facilities. They perform assays and establish and write specifications and standard operating procedures. Most people who fill this role have a BS. This position is often a good fit for job seekers who have backgrounds in science and like to work in highly structured settings.

Salary range: $39,000 to $60,000

CLINICAL RESEARCH PHYSICIAN

CRPs are MDs who develop and implement plans for ushering experimental drugs through preapproval clinical trials. They work on cross-functional teams to maximize understanding of the pharmacological, regulatory, and clinical dimensions of the drugs being studied.

Salary range: $90,000 to $200,000; company-sponsored speaking tours and other promotional events offer the enterprising physician numerous other ways to increase net income.

Engineering Jobs

A variety of engineering types—biochemical, chemical, electrical, environmental, industrial, mechanical, and software engineers—can find work in the industry. The roles an engineer can play are many and include everything from researching chemical compounds that can be turned into drugs to designing the manufacturing processes for those drugs once they've been developed.

Engineers, like scientists, encounter a dual ladder in this industry. Engineers can get promoted doing technical work or, if they have the aptitude and inclination, they can shift over at any point and become part of the management team that coordinates the work of the technical folks.

PROCESS ENGINEER

In most cases, process engineers work on project teams with more senior engineers. Job responsibilities may include designing chemical or biological methods for mass-producing compounds, designing equipment, and designing and overseeing the construction of various elements of manufacturing plants from pilot to commercial scale.

Salary range: $47,000 to $86,000

PROGRAMMER/ANALYST

These titles cover a wide variety of jobs, but put simply, programmers/analysts are computer people. There's a lot of complex database work to be done in this industry, particularly for clinical trials, which can involve thousands of patients (sometimes in several countries) with elaborate medical histories and completely different responses to each of the drugs and placebos being tested. And the computational demands of postgenomic research are enormous, creating demand for job seekers who have backgrounds combining science with computers. Bachelor's degrees are usually required (though not always).

Salary range: $43,000 to $86,000

Sales Jobs

Pharmaceutical companies employ a variety of people in different sales positions. Field sales reps call on doctors, hospitals, and HMOs. District managers usually manage ten to 14 field reps, hiring, training, and supervising them; area managers oversee the district managers. The act of selling to doctors is widely known as *detailing*, particularly if the salesperson uses company-produced visual aids. Reps service territories that are typically defined by both specialty and geography (e.g., all primary care doctors in Omaha, or all cardiologists in New Hampshire), and operate under a prescribed call cycle that determines how often they visit each doctor in their territory. Call cycles range between 2 weeks and 4 months for most drugs, but can sometimes be as short as a few days for hot new products or for physicians who are high-volume prescribers. Landing one of these jobs usually takes either a science background or some sales experience. Of the two, sales experience is decidedly more important.

Biotech sales is more intensive, since the products can be a hundred times more costly than the typical pharmaceutical drug. You need an interest in science to be able to discuss the products, but medical-business savvy is crucial. Biotech sales reps advise physicians on insurance reimbursement issues and the logistics of delivering the drug to patients. Consider the case of a pediatrician contemplating a $5,000 product. Salaries for pediatricians are on the lower end of the MD scale, so a five-dose purchase can run them a significant percentage of their annual salary. One insider describes the situation like this: "If the insurance company doesn't pay for it, that's a large expense. We have to have people who will hold the doctor's hand. We'll help qualify the patient [make sure she fits the protocol for insurance reimbursement], and we have programs to help the doctor with cash flow."

Biotech sales reps operate with more autonomy and less support from a sales manager. The pressure can be great. "In pharma, you're evaluated on the activity you generate, the number of calls, your selling skills," says an insider. "Here [in a biotech company] we never talk about that. You either get it [the sale] or you don't—and if you don't, you're out the door." But the rewards of biotech sales are as great as the risk. Base salaries and bonuses are greater than in pharma sales jobs, and stock incentives play a larger part.

SALES REP

Sales reps work with physicians, hospitals, HMOs, and countless other medical institutions to keep health-care professionals abreast of—and, if possible, partial toward—their company's line of products. Some of these jobs require extensive travel; others don't. A bachelor's degree in the sciences will help, but previous sales experience is more important in landing one of these jobs. Big Pharma companies have huge staffs of sales reps, so these positions can offer the necessary prerequisite for the more complex job of biotechnology sales, where salaries are higher and bonuses can exceed base salary.

Salary range: $32,500 to $76,000 plus incentives

Other Specialties

You don't need a science background to work in this industry, but it helps. People working in IT, HR, finance, or corporate communications must understand and be able to discuss their company's science and/or products.

Beginners in these fields are advised to look for a job in Big Pharma or a larger biotech company. "Start out big and work smaller and smaller," says one insider. "The big companies invest in training that the smaller companies don't have the excess infrastructure to carry off."

"At a start-up, you need to be able to perform," says a start-up biotech executive. "I look for someone to have done [the core responsibilities of the job] elsewhere two or three times." Once you prove yourself, you may be able to branch out into new areas in a smaller company, where staffs tend to be lean and the jobs aren't as well defined.

MARKETING ANALYST/ASSOCIATE PRODUCT MANAGER

Job seekers without a background in science can also find work on the marketing side in Big Pharma and large biotech companies. A marketing analyst is primarily responsible for coordinating and implementing campaigns for specific drugs, audiences, or both. This involves a little strategy and a lot of execution—things like developing collateral pieces, working as a liaison to advertising agencies, and overseeing a company presence at conventions. Many MBAs enter the industry this way, and—perhaps more important—few without MBAs move far beyond the marketing analyst level, although this varies from company to company. Other people come to these positions from sales.

Salary range: $38,000 to $75,000

PRODUCT MANAGER

This job requires managing a team of people and working to determine price, distribution, brand image, forecasting, and overall strategy for one or more drugs. On a micro level, the job can be claustrophobic: Imagine spending 13 months of 6-day weeks learning every aspect of a single drug, then having the company decide that it would be best simply to let the product die. But over the years you should be exposed to some of the most important, dynamic, and profitable drug markets in the industry, an experience that will give you a big-picture understanding of the industry and make you a greater asset to the company.

> **Start out big and work smaller and smaller. The big companies invest in training that the smaller companies don't have the excess infrastructure to carry off.**

Salary range: $60,000 to $100,000

REGULATORY AFFAIRS ASSOCIATE

The regulatory affairs career path suits job seekers who have a background in science but don't want to do lab work. A regulatory affairs associate completes the piles of paperwork required by the FDA. A BS is typically required; candidates without one may find themselves lost for several months. Those with a law degree come in at a higher level and with greater responsibilities, but with the same basic job description.

Salary range: $39,000 to $84,000

CLINICAL RESEARCH ASSOCIATE

These are the folks who oversee clinical trials. They get involved in designing protocols, enlisting physicians, training clinic personnel, and evaluating data. The job can require travel, sometimes as much as 80 percent of the time, but it doesn't always. CRAs may also manage the services of an independent clinical research organization that runs the actual studies. A BS or RN is typically required, or the equivalent in clinical experience.

Salary range: $42,000 to $95,000

MANUFACTURING TECHNICIAN

Technicians with high school diplomas operate equipment; weigh, measure, and check raw materials; maintain detailed records; and clean production areas. Associates with BS degrees implement procedures and get involved with scale-up, troubleshooting, and maintaining equipment. The industry is highly regulated by the FDA; manufacturing techs must comply with rigid standard operating procedures and good manufacturing practices.

Salary range: $24,800 to $54,000

Real People Profiles

Following are profiles of actual people working in the biotech and pharmaceuticals industry.

RESEARCH ASSOCIATE III

Years in business: 5
Age: 29
Education: BS in biology
Size of company: 5,000 employees
Hours per week: 45. The hours are pretty cushy. Once in a while I stay late or stop in on the weekend, but there are plenty of people who don't.
Annual salary/bonus: $56,000 plus options and benefits

What do you do?

I evaluate the ability of novel vaccines to improve the immune system.

How did you get your job?

Total, total networking. After I got out of school, I worked in an academic lab for a few years. When I decided I wanted to leave that job, my boss put me in touch with someone he knew here, and the guy gave me a job.

What are your career aspirations?

Within 5 years I'd like to be in grad school. I'm actually more interested in the policy side than the science side, so I'll probably end up studying public health or policy.

What kind of person does really well at this job?

A conscientious person—someone who pays attention to detail and questions why a thing is done a certain way, rather than assuming things are always fine the way they are.

What do you really like about your job?

My work has a purpose: the development of new medicines that will help people lead healthier lives. I really believe in what I do.

What do you dislike?

Corporate greed and politics often seem to override the philanthropic nature of my company's work.

What is the biggest misconception about this job?

That it's totally cutting-edge or really complicated. In 5 minutes, I can explain what I do to anyone.

How can someone get a job like yours?

Along with a college degree, you usually need some lab experience to get a job as a research associate. You can get this by working in a lab while you're in college. If you don't, you can get good experience by working as a medical technician in a hospital lab or a similar health-care setting.

Describe a typical day.

I usually spend about 3 days a week in the lab and 2 days a week in the office. Here's a lab day:

9:00   Come in and put on gloves, coat, goggles. Set up samples and start them running on a big machine.

1:00   Head down to the cafeteria for lunch.

2:00   Settle in to read the data off the machine that's running my experiment.

6:00   Go home.

Here's an office day:

9:00   The project this morning is to analyze the data I collected yesterday. I read my lab notes to see what I was looking for, and compare this with the data. The results are somewhat promising, and I create a few tables and graphs to represent the data.

12:00   Lunch at the cafeteria.

1:00   Write up a schedule for future experiments.

2:30   Take care of my inventory. Figure out what animals and supplies I'll need in the near future, and place the necessary orders.

5:00   Go home.

RESEARCH ENGINEER

Years in business: 2

Age: 25

Education: BS, MS in mechanical engineering

Size of company: fewer than 15 employees

Hours per week: 50; hours are pretty flexible, and weekend work is rare

Annual salary/bonus: $52,000 plus a performance bonus of around 10 percent

What do you do?

I design, build, and maintain robots and automated machinery for a small biotechnology company.

How did you get your job?

When I was finishing school, I decided that I wanted to get a job at a biotech company. One day I was chatting with my roommate's friend about my job search, and the guy told me that his cousin was a scientist at a biotech company that was looking for a mechanical engineer. I got in touch with him, he got me an interview, and I got the job.

What are your career aspirations?

I'm pretty happy here, but I think in a few years I'd like to try working in another industry to see what other challenges are out there.

What kind of person does really well at this job?

Someone who is a creative, persistent problem solver. It's easy enough to design and build a machine. The hard part comes when you've put it all together and it doesn't work. That's when you need to hang in there, think creatively, and come up with new ideas.

What do you really like about your job?

It's great to come up with a design and see it through to the creation of a working machine.

What do you dislike?

The grunt work. Machine maintenance—fixing broken valves, for instance—is something that I have to do a fair bit of, and it's really pretty boring.

What is the biggest misconception about this job?

I don't know; I think what I do is pretty straightforward.

How can someone get a job like yours?

Try to get networked in—go to conferences, talk to people you know who work in the industry. A science background is also a big plus.

Describe a typical day.

9:00   Come in, check e-mail, voice mail. A few new e-mails, no voice mail, no emergencies.

9:05   Walk down the hall to check on the synthesizers. These machines have been a big project of mine the whole time I've been here—I designed and built them from the ground up. Their purpose is to automate a key task that chemists formerly had to do manually. This morning I am making a few modifications—drilling holes, mounting hardware—that I hope will make the machines more reliable.

9:45   Explain the changes I've made to the chemists who work with the machines.

10:00   Back in my office. Unpack a box of parts that came in this morning. Make sure that my supplier sent me what I ordered. (He did.)

10:15   Research a pump I need to buy. Look on the Internet, call several vendors. Figure out exactly what I need; fill out paperwork for the order.

12:00   Go out to lunch at a nearby deli with a few biologists.

1:00   Work on putting together some new machines I'm building.

4:00   Meet with my company's other engineer and the scientist who is setting up a new lab to discuss the machines he's going to need.

5:00   The contractor who is building the electronics for my synthesizers comes in to do some testing. We discuss his timelines so that I can stay on top of any mechanical or electronic interface issues that might arise.

6:00   Go home.

SPECIALTY SALES REP

Years in business: 5 months
Age: 25
Education: BS in chemistry
Size of company: 20,000 people
Hours per week: 40
Annual salary/bonus: $45,000 plus $12,000 bonus and a company car

What do you do?

I visit doctors to educate them about the drugs my company sells. My goal is for them to prescribe my company's drugs.

How did you get your job?

I was working in research and decided that it wasn't where I wanted to go with my career, so I started looking for a job in sales. I spent about 5 months looking—answering ads in the paper, going through a recruiter, sending out unsolicited resumes, networking through friends. It took me a while to hone my interviewing skills. Then all of a sudden, everything just clicked, and I wound up getting a bunch of offers in a single week.

What are your career aspirations?

I don't have it all mapped out, but I definitely see sales as a stepping-stone to a management role, and it seems like there's a lot of possibility in my company.

What kind of person does really well at this job?

Someone who can deal confidently with the technical aspects of the job while being personable. You have to be able to interact with a wide range of personality types, from nice to nasty, and you have to be confident in your knowledge when you're dealing with doctors who don't want to see you or who think you don't know what you're talking about.

What do you really like about your job?

I like interacting with people all the time, and I love the freedom of my job. It's like owning my own business, and I know that if I work hard, I'll do well. I also like that what I do has a tangible, positive impact on my company's bottom line.

What do you dislike?

The honeymoon's still not over for me with this job, so I still like pretty much everything. But it seems like the lack of structure and supervision could definitely be a pitfall down the road.

What is the biggest misconception about this job?

That anyone can do it well. It is true that almost anyone can get by for a while, but in order to succeed, you really need to be serious about what you're doing. You need to be focused and determined, to stay on top of things at all times.

How can someone get a job like yours?

Sales experience is probably the most helpful thing. I didn't have sales experience, but I had a background in science, which was a plus, and I spent several months figuring out how to sell myself in an interview. Try to network your way into an interview. Look in the paper. If there aren't any ads for pharmaceutical sales reps, look again next week. You can also get a book called the PDR, the *Physician's Desk Reference*. It lists all the pharmaceutical companies in the country. I got this book and sent resumes out to about 90 companies, which got me about 20 interviews. In general, be confident and be patient.

Describe a typical day.

8:00   Get up, check voice mail. Two new messages—one's from my boss, to give me the weekly market share report; the other's from another sales rep to let me know that there's a particular study he's been pointing out to doctors that has been convincing them to prescribe one of our drugs. It's a good tip.

8:10   Plan out my day. There's a set group of doctors who are my responsibility, and I'm on a 2-week call cycle, which means I'm supposed to visit each one every 2 weeks. I sit down and look at who I'll be visiting that day, review my notes from my last visits, and figure out what my strategy will be with each doctor.

8:45   Hit the road.

9:00   Visit my first doctor of the day. Most doctors' offices are open from 9 a.m. to noon and again from 2 to 4 p.m. I try to hit five offices each morning. I don't always get in to see the doctors (which means I end up talking to the receptionist), but I'm getting better at it. A big part of the trick is just figuring out when to show up. I get in to see this guy, and do pretty well—I'm able to address some of the issues he mentioned during my last visit, and he seems mildly impressed.

9:30   Back on the streets. I manage to make it to four more doctors' offices by midday, though I only get in to see two of them.

12:00   Check voice mail, grab lunch, read a few new studies that have come out on the drugs I sell.

2:00   Back to the doctors. Of the five I'm visiting this afternoon, three are in the same building, which makes things pretty easy. I get in to see four of the five docs, which is nice, and I'm done with my day by 4 p.m., which is *really* nice.

4:05   Head home.

THERAPEUTIC SPECIALIST

Years in business: 3 (1½ in pharma sales; 1½ in current job in biotech sales)

Age: 30

Education: BS in nutrition with graduate work toward registered dietician and MBA

Size of company: 1,000 employees

Hours per week: more than 40, but hard to say because I work at home

Annual salary/bonus: $60,000 base plus $50,000 bonus (eligible for up to $85,000 bonus)

What do you do?

Consultative selling for a biotech product. I explain the product, identify patients, discuss how to use the product with a particular patient.

How did you get your job?

I was interested in pharmaceutical sales, but a headhunter said there was no way they'd hire me without sales experience. I went to a sales and marketing job fair and there were three pharma companies present. I was patient (there were a lot of people waiting to talk with them) and aggressive, and I closed them. Out of three interviews, I got three offers. After a year and a half, I was at the top of sales at the company, and a headhunter called me and I was able to move into a specialist position here.

What are your career aspirations?

My 5-year plan is to be in the home office as a product manager. Eventually I'd like to be a regional director.

What kind of person does really well at this job?

Someone who's outgoing and who reads people well. You have to know the signs: when it's time to go, when to step into the office, when to be stronger, and when to back off.

You need to be motivated because you're working out of your home. You need to be able to take rejection. It's a bummer.

What do you really like about your job?

The flexibility. The home office. Being out in the field. Some people think it's lonely, but I've developed such good relationships in the therapeutic community that I'm not lonely. The benefits are great. They give you a car and pay for all your gas.

What do you dislike?

The home office; it's hard to stop sometimes. The rejection and lack of respect for the sales profession.

What is the biggest misconception about this job?

People think pharma sales is easy, that you're always having lunch. It's not easy. My first year was very difficult, a really tough year. There's a lot of knowledge you need to have for this job. The average person couldn't do it.

How can someone get a job like yours?

Get to know people in the industry. Talk to people who have this job. General pharma sales positions are always available. There's high turnover. Once you're in, you're in.

Describe a typical day.

7:00   I work out of my home, so I am at my desk by 6:30 or 7:00 a.m. every day checking e-mail. I do a lot of business through e-mail—asking for appointments, answering questions. Then I might work on creating proposals until 8:30.

9:00   Out of the house.

10:00   Might have two appointments scheduled for the morning, and I might drop into one office. I prefer to work by appointment. I make appointments directly with the doctor rather than office staff because they make it difficult. They don't differentiate between a specialist and a general pharma rep.

12:00   Take a physician to lunch. Sometimes I bring lunch to their office, but I prefer to go out.

1:00   Two more appointments in the afternoon. Usually have only 5 to 10 minutes to discuss my product, but sometimes appointments last 45 minutes depending on the doctor's interest.

3:00   Drop into an office and the physician's on vacation, so I talk with the PharmD. I always sell directly to the doctor, but I talk to the members of the team. Both the PharmD and the nurse have a say. The nurse is around the patient a lot more than the doctor and reports on how the patient tolerates the drug, and the PharmD coordinates the meds and checks on how meds are working together. I also have a testing product so I talk to lab people about that.

4:00   Home again to check e-mail.

7:00   Take a physician out to dinner.

10:00   Home for the evening.

CLINICAL RESEARCH ASSOCIATE

Years in business: 1½ in industry after 3½ as a study coordinator in a clinic
Age: 39
Education: BA
Size of company: 800 employees
Hours per week: 45 to 50
Annual salary: $59,000

What do you do?

I manage all of the company's expanded access programs in the United States, Canada, Europe, and Australia for one particular compound currently in clinical trials. Expanded access is when the safety and efficacy of a drug has been sufficiently established and we're close to filing an NDA (new drug application) with the FDA, and we expand participation of a trial to include compassionate use by a sick population. It's a good-will gesture and also allows us to obtain data on a larger population.

How did you get your job?

Through a colleague who went to work for the company. Networking is everything.

What are your career aspirations?

I'm in line for a promotion to senior CRA. The next step is program manager; then comes associate director, which is probably as high as I can go because I'm not a clinician. What I really want to do when I grow up is be a therapist.

What kind of person does really well at this job?

Someone who communicates well both verbally and in writing. You have to be very organized and detail-oriented. There's so much paper, you're buried very quickly if you don't keep on top of it. Someone who has a very good memory. If you can keep a lot of things in your head and on the tip of your tongue, you'll do well.

What do you really like about your job?

That I work on the particular disease that I do. Also, I really like the people I work with. They're very open to questions. There are great mentors here. It's not a formal program; people are just very willing to help and teach, and my experience at the clinical site level is appreciated and respected.

What do you dislike?

The industry is pretty meeting-crazy. It makes it hard to get your job done. There are too many CCs on e-mails, and it makes for information overload. People need to have a better sense of what others really need to know. It's a huge time-waster when there's never enough time to begin with.

What is the biggest misconception about this job?

That you need to be a clinician and that you need industry experience. You don't. To get hired, what you need is a connection inside the company. Also, people think the work is glamorous because you get to travel a lot to monitor sites. It depends on the way the company works. We hire clinical data organizations to monitor the sites, so we don't travel much. At other companies CRAs might travel 75 to 80 percent of the time. It's important to know what the travel expectation is.

How can someone get a job like yours?

I knew a lot about the disease, not because I had a science background, but because of my clinical site experience. I would strongly suggest that you check with your college alumni association and set up informational interviews with people who do this work. There are now certificate programs for CRAs you can enroll in. Also, check the Web for local industry groups and consortia that hold regular meetings and presentations that anyone can attend. There are also industry conferences that you have to register and pay for, like the Drug Information Association and ICAAC (Interscience Conference on Antimicrobial Agents and Chemotherapy), which is part of the American Society for Microbiology.

Describe a typical day.

9:00   Check and return e-mail and voice mail. This can take 1 to 2 hours. I'm dealing with time differences, so I'm responding to a backlog of things that Europe has sent to me. Mondays are the worst, and today it took all morning.

12:00   We have a gourmet cafe on site, so I go there for a half-hour lunch. Then I take a walk around our lake.

1:00   Meet with my boss about a request I received from one of our investigators about an article he wants to write for publication about his experiences with our clinical trial. The guidelines for this process are laid out in his contract, but some clinical parts of the request were unclear, and we needed to discuss how much information we could supply to help him give an accurate account.

2:00   Attend the weekly group meeting where we share study updates and information.

3:00   Meet with my boss about a trial participant whose lab values have fallen out of range. When this happens, we might reduce the dosage or discontinue use. I'm not a clinician, so when it's really close, my boss, who's a PharmD, makes the call.

4:00   Attempt to meet with my other boss, but she's in a meeting that ran over so it doesn't happen. Then I check and return e-mail and voice mail until 6 p.m.

6:00   Go home.

DIRECTOR OF INTELLECTUAL PROPERTY

Years in business: 10
Age: 40
Education: PhD, JD
Size of company: 60 employees
Hours per week: 50 to 60
Annual salary: $140,000 plus stock options

What do you do?

I'm responsible for protecting our inventions. I oversee the company's patent estate. It's a one-person department, and we farm out most of the work to other lawyers. I read and revise patent applications and make sure they're valid and enforceable. I listen to the ideas of our scientists and make sure we get new invention disclosure forms completed in a timely fashion. Also, I research whether other people hold patents that may prevent us from developing or commercializing our new ideas. I review licensing agreements for in-licensing (when someone else has invented a technology that we want to develop) and for out-licensing (something we've invented that's not part of our core business that we want to sell). I try to follow the scientific, business, and patent literature closely with an eye to possible commercial partners and/or licensing opportunities. I participate in a variety of senior scientist meetings and provide input on patent implications of research. I also do trademark work involving naming our products and obtaining copyrights on written materials.

How did you get your job?

Through a friend of a friend. After I graduated from college, I taught high school chemistry, physics, and math for 2 years. Then I got a PhD in organic chemistry and went to work at a law firm. I went to a law firm rather than into research because I knew I was better at translating scientific concepts for nonscientists and nonscientific concepts for scientists. That seemed to be a better match for me than the straight, full-on, 100 percent science. The firm paid for night law school. During the day, I drafted highly technical patent applications. It meant some long hours.

But working for a law firm, I felt a little removed from the science. I missed being near a lab. Also, as a lawyer you're paid very well, but you don't have the upside potential of working for a start-up company. I came here more for the experience, and I took a cut in base pay. But there is potential for tremendous financial reward working for a bio-tech company. And now I'm 30 feet away from a lab. I have full access to the lab, so I can put on a pair of safety glasses and ask about an experiment or get some dry ice or pH paper. I no longer see the very challenging projects that get brought to a top-notch patent law firm, but here I can shape the science we're doing.

What are your career aspirations?

To become general counsel. The pay is greater, and the title is vice president, rather than director.

What kind of person does really well at this job?

Someone who is detail-oriented and likes working with paper. It's a blend of reading and interacting with people. You need efficient time management and clear writing and speaking skills. It also helps to be happy to go with the flow. I have definite things I have to do each day, but every day there's some sort of surprise or new development.

What do you really like about your job?

I love really good science. This company is small and has a very responsive management team. If I can come up with a compelling reason to do something, we can turn on a dime. Every day brings news in the press about us or a competitor. It's an exciting time for our area of development.

What do you dislike?

I miss the legal camaraderie. In a patent law firm of 250, there might be 40 to 50 people working in the biotechnology area. You get lots of legal feedback. Here I have to make do on my own. I try to make up for it by meeting other lawyers for lunch. Also, my commute is pretty awful.

What is the biggest misconception about your job?

For a scientist contemplating patent law and joining a law firm, the biggest misconception is that you're going to do science, or go to the library to research scientific questions—the grad school research idea that you're going to work on interesting science questions. Also, there are a lot of people who don't get it, that we're in the business to make money. At my current company, senior management is primarily business-trained as opposed to science-trained. A good part of my job is to make sure my department is cost-effective. We can't afford to file patents in every country.

How can someone get a job like yours?

You need to be an undergrad science major. An advanced degree helps, but isn't an absolute necessity. Go to law school. If you have a PhD, you don't need to worry so much about grades in law school. Just get the degree. But if you don't have a PhD, go to a top law school and get the best grades. Then work at the very best patent law firm you can. If you can't do that, get an internship at the patent office or at a university technology transfer program working on patent issues. Another route is if you are a biotech scientist. Take the patent agent exam and go to night law school and work your way up.

Describe a typical day.

6:55   Ride my mountain bike to train station and board Caltrain for a 1-hour commute. Reply to e-mail on my laptop and read the *New York Times* and the *Wall Street Journal.*

8:15   Arrive at office and prepare for a conference call with our CEO regarding a licensing issue for a joint venture.

9:00   Conduct the conference call.

10:00   Meet with a team from our bioinformatics group that is helping me assess some technology that we're going to license.

11:00   Interview a recent PhD candidate for our molecular biology group. My job isn't so much to assess knowledge of science. I'm involved on a personality-match level. Is this a smart, go-getting type of person?

11:45   Interview a candidate for director of protein chemistry who currently has a group of 20 people at another company. Is this person a good team player and a good manager?

12:30   Lunch at my desk

1:00   Attend a meeting to formulate a strategy on how to use our computer technology and information in the public domain to add value to our existing patent portfolio.

2:30   Review a draft agreement of a technology licensing agreement. Get notes and comments together for a conference with lawyers from the other side.

4:00   Walk over to a scientist to hound him for a write-up I need to put in a patent application.

5:00   Check e-mail. What's my day like tomorrow?

7:10   Back on Caltrain after bike ride from the office.

MANUFACTURING MANAGER

Years in business: 15
Age: 39
Education: MS in biochemistry
Size of company: 350 employees
Hours per week: 50
Annual salary: $100,000

What do you do?

I'm responsible for overseeing the day-to-day operations of one specific part of a pharmaceutical manufacturing plant.

How did you get your job?

It was listed on the company's website. I sent in my resume, but it also helped that I had friends who worked for the company.

What are your career aspirations?

I would like to manage the operation of an entire plant. That's the logical next step for this career path. Another option would be to switch to another department. Regulatory affairs is very interesting to me.

What kind of person does really well at this job?

People with good attention to detail. That orientation is key because it's a highly regulated industry. You also need good communication skills. There's a lot of written documentation. A science background is important but a mechanical inclination is just as important.

What do you really like about your job?

I get to work with people in different specialties. A lot of different groups interact with manufacturing. You can learn a lot about the organization.

What do you dislike?

Having to work with people who aren't team players. Teamwork is mandatory, and there are people who don't appreciate that.

What is the biggest misconception about this job?

A lot of people think it's like manufacturing cars. This isn't like heavy industrial manufacturing. This is science-related manufacturing. It's not mindless and it's not highly automated. Very skilled labor is required.

How can someone get a job like yours?

This is a good way to get into biotech. Schools don't teach biopharmaceutical manufacturing skills, so it's unreasonable for us to expect an entry-level worker to have them. We train people from scratch. We're looking for good communicators with mechanical aptitude and willingness to learn. The expectation is you'll work here for 2 to 4 years, then move on.

Describe a typical day.

7:00   The first thing I do is check to see what happened the night before. We're a 24-hour operation and I need to know where we are in production. Then I check e-mail and my calendar.

8:00   We have a daily start-up meeting to plan the day's activity.

9:00   Meet with the quality assurance group to investigate incidents.

10:00   Meet with one of the several supervisors who report to me.

11:00   Work on my own documents. We produce more paper than product.

12:00   Review batch records.

4:00   Meet with a plant engineer to review equipment specifications and construction schedule for a long-term facility expansion project.

5:00   Go home.

DIRECTOR OF OPERATIONS, PLANNING, AND ANALYSIS

Years in business: 6, all with the same company

Age: 37

Education: MBA

Size of company: well over 25,000 people

Hours per week: I'm pretty much an 8-to-6 guy and typically work a 50-hour week.

Annual salary/bonus: $180,000 including bonus, plus options

What do you do?

I spend about 50 percent of my time supervising a team of MBA analysts. My team is responsible for profitability forecasting, competitive analysis, analysis of large capital projects, mergers and acquisitions, and the financial aspects of the licensing and development projects. The team's findings are reported directly to senior management. The other 50 percent of my time is divided between high-level strategic planning projects and the preparation and delivery of presentations to senior management.

How did you get your job?

I worked as a summer associate here between my first and second years of business school. When I left that summer, the company made me an offer to return the following year as an analyst. I took them up on their offer, then worked my way up to senior analyst, and later to a position in business development, which in turn led into my current position.

What are your career aspirations?

I could see my career going in a number of directions. I could happily keep this job for several years to come. I could become a VP of a business unit or of corporate strategic planning. I could end up taking on a CFO role at one of my company's subsidiaries, or at an independent biotech company that's transforming itself from a lab-coat-and-petri-dish shop into a full-fledged, revenue-driven company.

What kind of person does really well at this job?

When people think of finance, they think of dull, repetitive jobs. And there are in fact lots of jobs like that. But there are also interesting, dynamic jobs. In order to work at interesting jobs, you need to be creative. You need to see the bigger picture, come up with fresh ideas, and throw yourself into the breach by creating projects and by taking on whatever comes your way. At the same time you need to pay attention to the details, to triple-check your data. No matter how beautiful or brilliant your presentation is, if there are errors in your data, they're all people will remember.

What do you really like about your job?

It is a high-stakes game that results in meaningful products. And the confluence of science and capital is incredibly interesting.

What do you dislike?

Corporate politics. I hate to see smart people become totally preoccupied with jostling for position. Also, I think there is too much functional segregation. Smart people can succeed anywhere and should get to rotate around more in the company. Too often people get pigeonholed and end up overinvested in one particular segment of the company.

What is the biggest misconception about your job?

That my team is made up of a bunch of police officers who exist solely to bust people's chops on behalf of senior management. In fact, we often work as a launching pad for new ideas and work collaboratively with people from all over the company.

How can someone get a job like yours?

Be a little bit unusual. Don't be afraid to jump into discussions, offer your own ideas, question other people's assumptions. Of course it takes some subtlety and tact, but this way you distinguish yourself from the mass of bodies, and you'll be able to take on interesting, innovative, valuable projects. It's also key to work for someone who appreciates you. And you in turn can help this process along by realizing that, particularly when you first come into the company, it's to your advantage to make your boss look good. Other key things to think about are your company's current needs and growth potential. Obviously, a company poised for dramatic growth will offer significantly more interesting opportunities than a company with a more stagnant outlook.

Describe a typical day.

8:00   Every morning from 8 to 8:30 my door is open to anyone who wants to drop by for an informal chat. This morning one of the MBAs on my analyst team comes by, and we talk over coffee about possibilities for her next job with the company.

8:30   Make the rounds. I like to manage by walking around, and I find the morning to be a good time to check in with each member of my team, see how projects are going, and help people troubleshoot any problems that are cropping up. Everyone seems to be on track this morning.

10:00   Meet with three analysts and four people from central research to discuss the status of our research on a company that is a potential acquisition target. I am scheduled to brief the CEO on the issue in 3 weeks and need to make sure that everyone's work is on track.

12:30   Go down to the cafeteria for lunch with several folks from the analyst team.

1:30   Desk time: return e-mails, voice mail.

2:00   Conference call with some folks on our European team. We're looking at forming an R&D alliance with a European biotech shop, and my group is responsible for performing the due diligence and for putting together the negotiating briefing documents.

3:00   Work on a presentation that I'm going to deliver to the CFO the day after tomorrow.

5:00   Make the rounds again. See if people are hitting their milestones. Make plans for tomorrow.

6:00   Go home.

SENIOR VICE PRESIDENT OF CLINICAL RESEARCH

Age: 47

Education: MD; currently completing an executive MBA

Certification: Board-certified in internal medicine, anesthesiology, and pulmonary medicine

Size of company: 55 employees

Hours per week: 70; weekdays 7 a.m. to 8 p.m., additional weekend hours

Annual salary: $240,000 plus stock options

What do you do?

I manage all clinical trial research, regulatory filings, and quality assurance for manufacturing and clinical trials. I also participate in R&D meetings for compounds being considered for clinical trials. I am a member of the senior management team.

How did you get your job?

I worked at a medical school and learned through my network of personal contacts that there were openings at this company. When I first came on, I worked part-time in clinical development and part-time in business development. I later moved over to full-time clinical development work, then up into senior management.

What are your career aspirations?

I try to wake up and do something interesting each day, and see where that takes me. What I'm doing now is a lot of fun, and I'd be happy to keep doing it for a while.

What kind of person does really well at this job?

A bright, self-motivated, independent person with a strong desire to succeed and an ability to learn quickly.

What do you really like about your job?

It's exciting, interesting, challenging, and worthwhile.

What do you dislike?

No matter how hard you work, there's always a high chance of failure.

What is the biggest misconception about this job?

People are naive about how incredibly difficult it is to bring a drug to market.

How can someone get a job like yours?

There are plenty of openings for MDs in biotech; the biggest step is usually deciding to give up clinical practice. For people who have made this decision, networking is usually the most effective means of landing a job.

Describe a typical day.

7:00   Come in. Work on revising standard operating procedures for clinical development protocols.

9:00   Develop presentation of new standard operating procedures for senior management meeting.

10:00   Senior management meeting.

12:00   Meet with members of the R&D team to discuss a compound moving out of R&D into clinical development.

1:30   Eat lunch at my desk; work on developing standard operating procedures for data management.

2:00   Meet with CEO to discuss a partnership we're developing with another company to jointly conduct preclinical research on a compound.

3:00   Conference call with MDs from two universities running clinical trials on one of my company's compounds.

4:00   Conference call with manufacturing partner.

5:00   Study quality assurance practices in manufacturing to prepare for tomorrow's meetings.

8:00   Go home.

The Workplace

Lifestyle

Culture

Diversity

Compensation

Insider Scoop

Lifestyle

Midsize and large companies offer the accoutrements of top-company corporate life: a comfortable salary, full benefits, and a well-funded work environment that often provides things like fancy subsidized cafeterias and plush in-house gyms. Indeed, most established companies in pharma and biotech are known for offering top-flight benefits—everything from on-site day care and generous family leave to tuition reimbursement and excellent professional development programs. Most insiders report tolerable work schedules that allow them to have a personal life.

The small biotech companies tend to lack the comfort and stability of the larger firms, though many insiders say the fun of the make-it-up-as-you-go-along ethos that prevails at small companies makes up for the lack of corporate opulence.

HOURS

Between 40 and 50 hours a week is the norm in the larger companies, and most people tend to choose traditional hours even when the company is receptive to flextime arrangements. An insider from a large biotech company says, "This place is dead by 6:00 every evening."

The same isn't always true in the smaller, more volatile biotech workplace. "There are crunch times, such as when we're presenting a drug to the FDA or during a merger, when we work a lot more hours," says one insider. "And you could say those events happen with regularity." As in every industry, there are people who work longer hours for reasons not necessarily dictated by the business, but generally this industry seems to understand that workers have personal lives.

TRAVEL

Travel varies widely in the industry. Sales reps with large territories are on the road every day. CRAs running clinical trials can travel as much as 80 percent of the time. Marketing analysts travel a good deal to maintain a company presence at industry meetings and to conduct focus groups. Most scientists travel less, although senior-level scientists may attend conferences and meet with far-flung colleagues.

Culture

Big Pharma companies are card-holding members of corporate America. People are "more collegial than in banking or consulting," says an insider, but still generally formal and businesslike. These are process-oriented firms—there's a right way and a wrong way to do most things, and your job is to do things the right way. There is also a clearly delineated hierarchy; people in this industry know who and what they are responsible for and to whom they have to answer. As another insider says, "Everything runs like clockwork, and you know what's expected."

Compared with Big Pharma, the biotech world is like the Wild West. The difference is partly geographical: With the notable exception of the thriving biotech scene in Cambridge, Massachusetts, most biotech action is in casual California. But there's more to the distinctions than time zones. Pharmaceutical companies know their game; the oldest of them have been playing it for a century. The biotech industry, on the other hand, is only a few decades old, which makes for a more improvisational workday, workweek, and work year. On a cultural level this translates into a democratic, free-thinking, chaotic, and often confusing workplace.

Biotech insiders say that change is the only constant, even in big biotech. "The company's mission is constantly in flux," says an insider. "Once you start generating revenue, there are pressures to be earnings-driven instead of scientifically creative. The company you came to work for is not the company you work for now."

Biotech companies also tend to be more casual and less stereotypically businesslike than pharmaceutical companies. Many biotech people look down their noses at Big Pharma.

Across the biotech-pharma spectrum, industry culture tends to be rather brainy, a function of the fact that it is an industry driven by a highly intellectual research process. In addition, most people in these industries really believe in what their company does and genuinely feel that they are helping to make the world better.

Diversity

As corporate America goes, this industry is pretty good. An unusually high number of foreign-born employees—particularly on the science side—gives the industry a cosmopolitan flavor. Nevertheless, the industry is still mostly run by white males, and domestic-partner benefits are rare.

But Big Pharma is well-represented on *Working Mother* magazine's widely respected list of the "100 Best Companies for Working Mothers," mainly because of excellent family-oriented benefits. The 2004 list included 14 biotech and pharma companies: Abbott Laboratories, AstraZeneca, Aventis, Bristol-Myers Squibb, Eli Lilly, GlaxoSmithKline, Johnson & Johnson, Novartis, Pfizer, Schering-Plough, and Wyeth.

Compensation

Base salaries in pharma and biotech seem comparable. Surprisingly, the smaller companies sometimes pay more than their larger counterparts to compete for talent. "Sometimes the little guys have to pay more to attract people because they don't have the name," says one HR executive. And because biotech companies in California must compete with Silicon Valley for staff, salaries there tend to be higher than elsewhere in the country.

Perhaps the biggest difference between large and small company compensation is in bonuses and benefits. The larger companies (both pharma and biotech) are more likely to pay cash bonuses, match 401(k) contributions, and offer stock purchase plans. Biotech companies that don't yet have revenues to match such perks are more generous with stock options. While stock options are no longer expected to compensate for below-market-rate base pay, at the right company (read: one that gets a drug to market), they can ultimately pay off in a big way.

Individual performance bonuses are common at all levels. Some companies also have team-based performance bonuses. Signing bonuses and relocation bonuses can also enter the picture, depending on the company and the candidate. Though hefty packages are more standard with Big Pharma and big biotech, any company located in high cost-of-living zones like the San Francisco Bay Area will tend to be more open to creative relocation negotiations, though relocation bonuses have been harder to come by in recent years.

Three weeks of vacation per year is typical, and after a few years, 4 weeks is not uncommon. And unlike companies in some other industries, pharmaceutical and biotech companies encourage their employees to actually take their vacation days—as long as they don't schedule them during an FDA plant inspection, the due-diligence period before an acquisition, or some other critical activity.

Insider Scoop

WHAT EMPLOYEES REALLY LIKE

Changing Lives

Most people in this industry believe deeply in what their company does. As one MBA says, "When you're in the pharmaceutical industry, yeah, you're there to make money, but there's also the underlying fact that you're doing something that is going to make a huge difference in thousands of people's lives."

The Good Life

Although there's some debate as to whether industry scientists work fewer hours than their academic colleagues, they most certainly earn more. And they don't have to hustle for money. "It's nice not always having to worry about funding," says one insider. For their part, MBAs can hit six figures not long after coming out of school without suffering through the travel and long hours imposed on classmates who opt for consulting or banking.

That Guy's Pretty Sharp

"A lot of brilliant people are attracted to this industry," says one recruiter. And while many of these industrial-strength geniuses are attracted by the research opportunities, it's often the presence of fellow thinkers that they find most enjoyable. "It is definitely a more intellectual industry than most, which is great," says one insider.

Choose Your Own Adventure

If you like having the rules spelled out and an obvious career ladder, sign on with Big Pharma. If, on the other hand, you don't think you can take the hierarchy but don't want to give up the perks of a large company, try a large biotech. If you want to be on a first-name basis with the CEO, a start-up is the place for you. It's all here. You decide.

WATCH OUT!

Business First

In the final analysis, the companies that comprise this industry are just that: companies. Their chief aim is to maximize profits, not save lives, and this goal is reflected in the decisions they make. If you end up working on the world's 13th drug for high blood pressure instead of the world's first drug to treat some incurable disease, don't say we didn't warn you.

Consolidation Blues

"There's always the risk of layoff," says an insider. "I don't care who you are [Big Pharma or start-up biotech]." While the pharmaceuticals industry is less volatile than it was a few years ago, mergers and acquisitions are always a possibility. Job security is no longer assured, particularly if you're in administration or manufacturing. While your experiences will likely serve you well in finding a new job in the industry, no one enjoys being laid off. And a merger can be an adjustment even if you keep your job. "Every time you turn around it seems you have a new title and you're still sitting at the same desk," says a veteran of three consolidations.

The Living Dead

The vast majority (5,999 of every 6,000) of promising compounds fail to develop into a marketable drug. So if you're working for a small biotech company, there's a serious possibility that your company's efforts will never produce a marketable product, which in turn would transform the small, vibrant company you joined into a stagnant mire. If you're considering a stint with a biotech shop, evaluate its prospects as thoroughly as possible, and heed an insider's warning: "You don't want to end up among the living dead."

The MS Shuffle

"A few people without PhDs make it to scientist, but the vast majority [with a BS or MS degree] hit a ceiling at the research specialist level, between 5 and 10 years into their career," says one veteran of industry labs. For many people this is fine—it's a comfortable, reasonably well-paid job that allows for a healthy work/life balance. But if you have grand career ambitions and want to stay in science—and don't have a PhD—you may find more frustration than fulfillment here.

Keep Me in the Loop

Because work is done in teams, there are a lot of meetings. One recruiter's advice to scientists, "You won't just be working at the bench," might be considered an understatement for the kind of interaction required. And one fallout of the attempt to keep team members informed is a tendency to err on the generous side when copying people on memos. "I get 200 e-mails a day," says one insider. "And the majority, I don't need to see." While the same could be said about many industries, the situation is aggravated by the tremendous volume of documentation required in the highly regulated climate of biotech and pharma.

Getting Hired

The Recruiting Process

Interviewing Tips

Getting Grilled

Grilling Your Interviewer

The Recruiting Process

Recruiting practices vary widely from company to company. In general, on-campus recruiting accounts for a very small part of the industry's overall recruiting activity. Companies normally recruit at a few target schools, and only for selected positions. The target schools might include a core set of business schools for positions in marketing and finance and a core set of colleges for BS and MS scientists and engineers.

If you interview with a company that is recruiting at your school, you're likely to have your first interview on campus. This is a screen to see whether your skills and personality fit the general type the company is looking for. If the company is interested in you after the first round, you're usually invited to interview at its headquarters with all travel expenses paid. If you go to headquarters, expect a long day—you'll probably have somewhere between five and ten interviews with your would-be boss, folks in human resources, your would-be coworkers, and, often, your would-be boss's boss. The company will probably offer you a job—or not—on the spot.

If the company or companies that interest you don't recruit on your campus (or if they recruit on your campus, but for the wrong type of job), you'll need to take some initiative. This can take many forms, but one of the best is networking. "If you can make a personal connection inside a company, you'll be way ahead of the game," says one insider. In addition to friends and family members, college graduates should consider using their alumni associations to find alums in the industry from whom they can request an informational interview. In rare cases, a helpful alum can help you find a job outright; more often, he or she will help you target your search and connect you with the right people. Former professors—particularly those closely connected to the industry—are another valuable networking resource.

Many companies have comprehensive and up-to-date job listings posted on their websites, and most let you apply online. Even if you don't apply for one of these jobs, looking at several sites can give you a good idea of what's going on in terms of industry hiring (or at least a specific company's hiring).

Don't overlook the want ads. "If there aren't any listings for sales reps in the newspaper this week," says one field sales rep, "there'll be some next week." Good online resources include BioSpace.com, Medzilla.com, Jobscience.com and Bioview.com. Scientists should look in the classified sections of journals like *Science* and *Nature,* both of which have online versions.

Whatever strategy you use, be persistent. It may take you several months to land a job, but if you find a good one, it will be time well spent.

UNDERGRADS/MASTERS

Some larger firms have rotation programs for top candidates coming straight out of college. These programs typically rotate fresh-faced recruits through 4- to 6-month assignments over the course of 2 years. Examples include Merck's Manufacturing Management Development Program for science and engineering grads and Johnson & Johnson's Financial Leadership Development Program for college grads with business backgrounds. Rotational programs are a fantastic way to learn about the industry and make it onto the radar screens of all the right people. To find out if a specific company has a rotation program, visit its website or contact its college recruiting department.

Several insiders recommend industry-oriented temp agencies as an excellent way for BS/MS holders who want to work in R&D or QA/QC to get a foot in the door. Agencies include Lab Support, BioSource, and Kelly Scientific. Many of these jobs are temp-to-perm, which means you might wind up with a full-time position in an industry lab.

Another good entry point for biotech is manufacturing. "You may wonder why you went to school for 4 years," says an industry recruiter, "but it's a proving ground." Science-based biotech manufacturing requires a highly skilled labor force, but since you can't learn the specific skills in school, companies will train you from the ground up. And you'll get the kind of exposure you need to move into other areas that interest you.

If you don't have a technical background or mechanical aptitude, your best ticket into the industry is as a pharmaceutical sales rep. You'll be told you need sales experience, but there are plenty of insider reports of getting hired without it. If you're interested in biotech sales, pharma sales experience is a must. "We look at pharma as a stepping stone," says a biotech insider. "We would never hire a sales rep straight from another field."

MBAS

Several Big Pharma companies offer rotational programs for top candidates graduating from business school. These programs move participants through 6-month shifts at a variety of organizational functions—sales, marketing, finance, operations—and serve as an institutional fast track for top management prospects. A summer job between the first and second years of business school often serves as a tryout for a company's rotational program.

But most MBAs aren't hired into rotational programs; they're more likely to find jobs in marketing and finance. MBAs looking for jobs in business development may have to wait a couple of years. "Business development people need a fat Rolodex," says one insider, "and it takes a while to build one up."

PHDS

PhDs should have at least one scientific publication under their belts, preferably as first author, and should have completed a postdoc. Beyond those requirements, finding a lab that does what you do is the central task. Networking and classified ads are the best options.

MDS

Most of the jobs in the industry are for specialists. It's very uncommon to get hired straight out of a residency; most hires need to have some clinical practice experience. Any experience as a clinical investigator is a big plus.

Interviewing Tips

1. Technical folks should be ready to demonstrate that they can apply what they've learned in school. "If a candidate who's taken some chem courses can't tell us how to make a 1-molar solution of a given reagent," says one insider, "It's a very bad sign." This may mean you'll need to spend some time before your interview reviewing some of those textbooks you haven't looked at since freshman year.

2. Before you go into the interview, think about the nature of the company and the type of person who's likely to thrive there. Chances are good that a small biotech company will want someone who can handle uncertainty and wear a lot of hats, while a huge pharmaceutical company will be looking for someone who does things by the book. Be honest about your capabilities, but give some thought as to how to present yourself in the best light.

3. Particularly for nontechnical people, it's key to have general knowledge of the industry and specific knowledge of the company you're interviewing with. For company information, a company's website is a very good place to start, but you'll get a broader perspective if you can find an objective third-party source. This guide is a good start for general knowledge; to go a little deeper, check out the recommended reading in "For Your Reference." Here are a few things you should know before the interview: What are the company's leading drugs and/or therapeutic areas? What does the company pride itself on? What does its pipeline look like? If it's a diversified company, what are its nonpharmaceutical businesses? Where is the company headquartered? What distinguishes it from others in the pack?

4. If you're applying to work in a lab, learn as much as you can about the work that goes on there. If you've done very similar work, you're in great shape. If not, studying up on your would-be lab's specialty is a great way to prepare for your

interview. Find out the name of the PhD who runs the lab, and do a search to see if she has published anything recently. If she has, read it!

5. Behavioral interviewing is popular in the industry, particularly for nontechnical positions. In a behavioral interview, the interviewer asks for examples of experiences when you demonstrated certain traits. "Give an example of a time you took a leadership role," is a classic behavioral interview question. If you're applying for a nontechnical position, spend some time before your interview thinking about your work, school, and extracurricular experiences. Make a few mental notes of moments or anecdotes that might prove relevant to behavioral interview questions.

6. Be team oriented. Most of the work that goes on in this industry is collaborative, and the people hiring you will want to make sure you can work this way. Not only do scientists need the right credentials, recruiters look for the ability to communicate well. You won't be exclusively working at the bench—you'll probably serve on teams with people from marketing, finance, engineering, and manufacturing. This is also important for MDs, who often must fight against the stereotype that they are hyperindividualists who can't work as part of a team.

7. If you can't answer a question, say so. In the words of the director of college recruiting at a leading pharmaceutical company, "'I don't know' is a perfectly acceptable answer to some questions."

8. If you're not sure you understand what your interviewer is asking, don't be afraid to say so. It's much better to have the interviewer rephrase a question than to squander your valuable interview time answering the wrong question.

9. Stay calm. This is a big industry, and if this company doesn't hire you, you can find another one that will.

Getting Grilled

Some interviewers work from a script, others wing it, and still others tailor their questions to your particular background. Here are some things they might ask:

- Why do you want to work in this industry? (Try to think of something besides the part about saving lives—which is not to say that you shouldn't mention it, but rather that if you mention that and something else, you're more likely to make a lasting impression.)

- Where do you see yourself 5 years down the road?

- Give me an example of a time you took a leadership role.

- Give me an example of a time you worked as part of a team to accomplish a goal.

- Scientists: Take a few minutes right now to think of a few technical questions that your interviewer might ask you based on your coursework or previous lab experience.

Grilling Your Interviewer

Here are some good questions to ask your interviewer. Not all of them may apply to you, but most are of general interest to anyone choosing an employer, and we have listed some of special importance to both engineering and nonengineering candidates. The questions assume you will have already covered basic topics like compensation and benefits packages.

FOR EVERYONE

- How do you see the industry changing over the next 5 (10) years?

- What distinguishes (company name) from (competitor name) or (competitor name)?

- What types of career opportunities could this job lead to?

- What are your favorite and least favorite things about this job/company?

FOR A PHARMACEUTICAL COMPANY

- Is the company involved in any biotechnology research or alliances with biotech?

- Did industry consolidation of several years ago affect the company? If so, What impact do you think it will have in the next few years?

FOR A BIOTECH COMPANY

- How is this company funded? What partnering agreements does it have? What are the upcoming milestones and at what point will additional financing be required?

- When might you realistically see (this small biotech company) making an IPO?

- Is the company profitable? When does the company expect to be profitable?

For Your Reference

Industry-Speak

Books

Online Resources

Industry-Speak

Every industry has its own argot; pharmaceuticals and biotechnology are no exception. The definitions that follow are designed merely to get you started; we don't pretend that they're comprehensive.

Action letter. Letter from the Food and Drug Administration (FDA) announcing a decision by the agency.

Approval letter. Type of FDA action letter that allows a drug to go to market.

Biochip. Semiconductor made with organic material.

Bioinformatics. The management and analysis of biological research data using advanced computing techniques. Particularly important in genomics research because of the large amount of complex data generated.

Bioprocessing. The use of living cells or the molecules involved in creating them (usually, enzymes) to make desired products (e.g., yeast).

Breakthrough drug. A drug that offers a dramatic step forward in terms of efficacy, side effects, dosing, or price; Claritin and Viagra are recent examples. Breakthrough drugs often get coverage on the evening news or talk shows.

Clinical trial. Four phases of rigorous testing conducted to establish a drug's safety and efficacy in humans. Phase I tests a tiny group of healthy people to determine the safe dosage range and track how the drug is metabolized by the body. Phase II tests a mid-size group of patients who actually have the condition targeted by the prospective drug. Phase III increases the test group to more than a thousand patients and uses a double-blind, placebo-controlled protocol. If a drug is clearly more effective than the placebo and causes no serious adverse events, the manufacturer submits a new drug application (see below). Phase IV is a postmarketing study done after drug approval.

Cloning. The production of genetically identical molecules, cells, plants, or animals.

Contract research organization. A CRO oversees the clinical trials required for FDA approval of a drug.

Contract sales organization. A CSO helps sell and market drugs for companies that lack the resources to do it themselves.

Detail. Usually a verb in pharmaceutical sales. To detail is to provide a doctor with information about a product, particularly with the help of a company-produced visual aid.

Direct-to-consumer (DTC) marketing. Prescription drug advertising that targets laypeople rather than physicians. This is the hottest segment of industry marketing.

Drug delivery. How a drug is administered (e.g., nasal spray, intravenous injection, suppository, capsule or liquid meant for oral ingestion).

Ethical pharmaceuticals. Products, including biological and medicinal chemicals, used to treat disease in humans or animals, promoted mainly to health-care professionals. This category may include both over-the-counter and prescription drugs.

Formulary. A managed-care company's list of reimbursable drugs. When a patented drug goes off patent, it is usually kicked off the formulary in favor of a cheaper generic.

Generic (or off-patent) drug. Once the patent on a drug expires, anyone can manufacture and sell it. An entire generic drug industry does precisely that, and since generic drug companies have no R&D costs to cover, they can sell the drug at a 50 to 90 percent discount.

Genomics. The study of genes and their functions. Genomic research is revolutionizing our understanding of the molecular mechanisms of disease and revealing thousands of new biological targets for drug development.

Genotype. Genetic makeup of a single person or a group of people.

Good manufacturing practices. GMPs are manufacturing regulations established by the FDA that require companies to extensively document their ongoing manufacturing efforts. If you work in quality assurance or quality control, GMPs will exert a large influence over your life.

Investigational new drug application. When a company is ready to begin testing a drug on humans, it submits an IND application to the FDA, which then has 30 days to accept or reject it. If the application is accepted, the company proceeds with Phase I through III clinical trials.

Isogenic. Belonging to the same genotype.

Microarray. An array of DNA or protein molecules on thousands of slides to create DNA or protein "chips." Allows the analysis of thousands of samples simultaneously.

Monoclonal antibodies. Highly targeted protein molecules that attack specific diseased or infected cells. Currently a hot area full of promise for biotech companies.

Nanobiotechnology. The study and use of tiny structures and machines created using as little as a single molecule.

New drug application. A company's final FDA application to sell a prescription drug. It is not uncommon for an NDA to be 50,000 pages long; FDA review typically takes 1 to 2 years unless the drug treats a life-threatening illness or one that has no effective pharmacological treatments. In such cases, the FDA often gives the application a priority review, sometimes cutting the review time in half.

Over-the-counter drug. A drug that can be sold directly to consumers, without a prescription. Most new OTC drugs started out as prescription drugs.

Patented drug. A drug that is under patent to a pharmaceutical company. A patent on a drug lasts for 20 years. When it runs out, competitors can produce and sell the drug as a generic.

Pipeline. A company's collection of drugs in development. Since drugs are patented for only 20 years—and it can take a decade or longer to bring a drug to market—pipeline strength is a key predictor of a company's success.

Pharmacogenomics. The study of how one's genetic inheritance affects the body's response to drugs. The idea is that drugs might one day be tailor-made for individuals and adapted to each person's own genetic makeup. Pharmacogenomics combines biochemistry with knowledge of genes, proteins, and single nucleotide polymorphisms.

Pharmacokinetics. The study of how drugs move through the body and the way they are affected by biological processes of uptake, distribution, elimination, and biotransformation.

Proteomics. The study of proteins and their post-translational modifications, considered to hold the key to curing gene-based diseases.

Quality control/quality assurance. The folks who work in this area make sure that drugs are manufactured in accordance with FDA regulation. Note to scientists: Don't limit yourselves to R&D—opportunities abound in QA/QC.

Recombinant DNA. Think of it as DNA that has been combined with other DNA and then replicated. It's made by putting foreign DNA, such as bacteria or yeast, into the DNA of an organism so that the foreign DNA is replicated along with the host DNA.

Snips. The genomic term for single nucleotide polymorphisms, or SNPs.

Stem cells. Undifferentiated cells that are able to be separated from the just-days-old conglomerations of cells called *blastocysts*, which eventually develop into embryos. Stem cells can differentiate into any type of cell in the body, and so have tremendous research potential, but cloned stem cells are the subject of tremendous political controversy; the Bush administration has placed restrictions on stem-cell research using federal funds.

Xenotransplantation. Transplantation of nonhuman animal species' cells, tissues, or organs into humans.

Books

From Alchemy to IPO: The Business of Biotechnology

Cynthia Robbins-Roth (HarperCollins, 2000)
Written by a long-time industry insider and founding editor-in-chief of BioWorld
Publications, this is an informed prediction of the industry's impact on the 21st century,
in terms of both innovation and moneymaking potential. "The biotech world will
never be an easy place for investors," writes Robbins-Roth, "but with hundreds of
ongoing projects poised to power into the marketplace, there will be plenty of opportunities for investors and employees alike."

Biotechnology Unzipped: Promises & Realities

Eric S. Grace (National Academy Press, 1997)
A palatable and entertaining explanation of a complex scientific topic that also includes
a discussion of ethical repercussions and public concerns. The author uses common
metaphors to describe genetic code to the layperson.

The Billion-Dollar Molecule: One Company's Quest for the Perfect Drug

Barry Werth (Touchstone Books, 1994)
This fine (if a bit dated) chronicle of the Cambridge, Massachusetts, firm Vertex
Pharmaceuticals has already established itself as a classic of business literature. Werth is
extremely fluent with the intricate scientific and financial obstacles that dictate the mores
of pharmaceutical development. He reveals the tale of Vertex's attempts to develop a
new immunosuppressant using biotech concepts and pharma-company cash. Werth
also conveys the thrill of discovery—racing against competitors to prove and then pub-
lish the latest clinical findings—as well as the all-or-nothing sense of doom that often
stems from everyday bad luck. No book in print offers such an exemplary insider's
account of drug development and its unique culture.

Your Complete Guide to Getting a Pharmaceutical Sales Job

Lisa Alexander (PRS Publishing, 2003)

Information to help you land and ace interviews for sales-rep positions.

Be Bright. Be Brief. Be Gone:
Career Essentials for Pharmaceutical Representatives

David Currier (iUniverse, 2001)

A thorough guide to what it's like to be a pharma sales rep, plus tips on how to sell pharma products effectively.

Introduction to Bioinformatics

Teresa Attwood and David Parry-Smith (Prentice Hall, 2001)

A guide to the burgeoning field of bioinformatics—of interest to biologists, computer scientists, and anybody else who'll be working in this field. Includes access to interactive online information.

Jobs in the Drug Industry: A Career Guide for Chemists

Richard Friary (Academic Press, 2000)

Tons of information for chemists, especially organic chemists.

Online Resources

Med Ad News

An outstanding resource for the industry novice, *Med Ad News* (www.pharmalive.com/ magazines/medad) is written for the advertising industry about the drug industry. The site it's on, PharmaLive.com, is also chock full of news about the industry.

BioSpace.com

This website is a comprehensive source of daily biotech and pharmaceutical news, stock quotes, company profiles, jobs, and industry events. BioSpace is the most likely place for a biotech company to list jobs online outside its own company website.

PhRMA

The Pharmaceutical Manufacturers of America is a leading trade organization and its website (www.phrma.org) is a good, if biased, source for information on industry statistics, policies, developments, and players.

Biotechnology Industry Organization

BIO's excellent website (www.bio.org) includes a downloadable guide to biotech careers that will be particularly useful to entry-level job seekers.

The American Society for Microbiology

This organization (www.asm.org) claims the oldest and largest single life-science membership in the world, and sponsors industry meetings including the Interscience Conference on Antimicrobial Agents and Chemotherapy, a useful networking opportunity for those in clinical development. Membership is $53.

Drug Information Association

Check www.diahome.org for clinical development jobs and industry internships.

OTHER INFORMATIVE WEBSITES

- www.bioinform.com

- www.sciencemag.org

- www.pharmaceuticalonline.com

- www.bioview.com

- www.inpharm.com

WETFEET'S INSIDER GUIDE SERIES

Job Search Guides

Getting Your Ideal Internship

Job Hunting A to Z: Landing the Job You Want

Killer Consulting Resumes!

Killer Cover Letters & Resumes!

Killer Investment Banking Resumes!

Negotiating Your Salary & Perks

Networking Works!

Interview Guides

Ace Your Case: Consulting Interviews

Ace Your Case II: 15 More Consulting Cases

Ace Your Case III: Practice Makes Perfect

Ace Your Case IV: The Latest & Greatest

Ace Your Case V: Return to the Case Interview

Ace Your Case VI: Mastering the Case Interview

Ace Your Interview!

Beat the Street: Investment Banking Interviews

Beat the Street II: I-Banking Interview Practice Guide

Career & Industry Guides

Careers in Accounting

Careers in Advertising & Public Relations

Careers in Asset Management & Retail Brokerage

Careers in Biotech & Pharmaceuticals

Careers in Brand Management

Careers in Consumer Products

Careers in Entertainment & Sports

Careers in Health Care

Careers in Human Resources

Careers in Information Technology

Careers in Investment Banking

Careers in Management Consulting

Careers in Marketing & Market Research

Careers in Nonprofits & Government Agencies

Careers in Real Estate

Careers in Retail

Careers in Sales

Careers in Supply Chain Management

Careers in Venture Capital

Industries & Careers for MBAs

Industries & Careers for Undergrads

Million Dollar Careers

Specialized Consulting Careers: Health Care, Human Resources,
and Information Technology

Company Guides

25 Top Consulting Firms

25 Top Financial Services Firms

Accenture

Bain & Company

Booz Allen Hamilton

Boston Consulting Group

Credit Suisse First Boston

Deloitte Consulting

Deutsche Bank

The Goldman Sachs Group

J.P. Morgan Chase & Co.

McKinsey & Company

Merrill Lynch & Co.

Morgan Stanley

UBS AG

WetFeet in the City Guides

Job Hunting in New York City

Job Hunting in San Francisco